To Pete –
with continuing gratitude
for your interest and great
to reconnect again.
D–

All in the Name of the Bible

Selected Essays on Israel and American Christian Fundamentalism

All in the Name of the Bible

Edited by
Hassan Haddad and Donald Wagner

AMANA BOOKS

We dedicate these essays to all the Children of Abraham, Jews, Muslims and Christians alike, who tenaciously hold to seeing each person as an equal Child of God, and who steadfastly resist all false prophets and pseudo-biblical teachings that would have us think otherwise.

ISBN 0-915597-42-X

AMANA BOOKS
58 Elliot Street
Brattleboro, Vermont 05301

Produced by Maple Leaf Press
Brattleboro, Vermont

CONTENTS

Introduction

A self-fulfilling prophesy is a prediction which comes true not because of the inevitable unfolding of history, but because of the power of the prediction itself. It is an event which transpires after the effort of its forewarners. Such events, fear the editors of this volume, are those being hailed today by many of the proponents of religious fundamentalism. Whether it is an attempt to find in one narrow reading of holy writing a legal order for the righteous society; or justification for the colonial oppression of a native people in their own land; or the perfect blueprint for the cataclysmic end of history, Biblical fundamentalism is always the single-minded defense of a particular and supposedly clear and unquestionable reading of religious scripture. In the name of literalism, it is often the promotion of obscurity and intrigue in the text, a puzzle only to be calculated by a mystical elite. By organizing social support for the very historical intrigue it foretells, this elite claims divine knowledge.

It is our contention in this volume, the expanded second edition, that the resulting politics of contemporary Biblical fundamentalism are not only hermeneutically unsound, but are so dangerous that they encourage the very international and interracial confrontation they prophesy: a nuclear Armageddon. In the name of the Bible, a sympathy for the Apartheid regime in South Africa becomes a moral requirement. In the name of the Bible, a total commitment to Israel's militancy is required as an article of Biblical faith. In the name of the Bible, the divined and created "holy" mysteries of terror, international conflict, and war become more inspiring to the faithful than a Biblical mandate to compassion, decency, or the love of neighbor.

Biblical fundamentalism is not new. Yet it has, in recent years, taken a fervor reminiscent of its previous appearances during times of social and political upheaval. The Crusades, the religious wars of the Reformation, and spread of colonialism, especially of settler colonial practices in the Americas, Australia, and Africa, including the extermination of the Amerindians, the resurgence of slavery in the New World, and the colonization of Africa, all are events that occured, perhaps not coincidentally, with the rise of religious fundamentalist movements. All were condoned and promoted in the name of the Bible.

There is ample evidence of the many uses to which the Bible, in particular, has been put. While it has marshalled opposition to injustice and oppression through history, it has also been used as uncritical defense of intolerance, of brute power, and to add divine legitimacy to exclusivist and expansionist political designs. The Bible has, for many, justified a scorecard which identifies the good and the "evil empires," promising the vindication of the victors by the Lord's strong hand. History has felt the comings and goings of such dogma.

The present wave of Biblical fundamentalism however, is, we feel, uniquely privileged and uniquely dangerous. For three unprecendented elements converge. First is the coincidental heating up of fundamentalist rhetoric in all three Biblical religions. Contemporary religious Revisionists within Zionism, for one, are gaining political and persuasive influence in the Middle East and throughout the West with their celebration of a Jewish ethnic privilege in the identified Biblical land and its advocacy of a "return" to a political order of things that existed in Biblical times. Both of these are to be culminated by the completed "return" of the Jews to an ethnically purified Promised Land.

Khomeinism, the most extreme but not the sole movement of Islamic fundamentalism, aims at the "restoration" of the "pure" Islamic state and the rule of unchangeable and unquestionable sacred law. It gains political influence and adherants in frustrated and crisis-filled lands.

To compliment, Christian fundamentalism, particularly in the United States, looks forward to a "restoration" of a version of the Biblical city. Although such social transformation is seen to be ordained by God, the faithful need still to be active in promoting it, hastening its coming, and "watching the signs."

The fundamentalist movements may disagree on the nature and scope of their goals. However, many of their adherents agree on three things: the absoluteness of their beliefs, the exclusiveness of truth within these beliefs, and either the acceptance or justification of violent means to reach the "restoration."

The second factor which prompts our concern with contemporary fundamentalism is the privilege and marvel of modern media. Symbols are created, ideas processed, and the message propagated more easily and quickly than ever before. And the one-way nature of modern mass media is especially appropriate to the highly concentrated and defined view of authority inherent in the fundamentalist message. Fundamentalism teaches, it does not converse or enter dialogue. And truth, to be sure, is not the mutual discovery of respectful partners, but is the possession of the teacher. Electronic and symbolic media, therefore, become easy tools for such messages.

Khomeini's revolution was in part due to the efficiency and usefulness of the cassette tape player. The able use of television and radio by Christian fundamentalists in the United States in the past decade has amounted to one of the most elaborately conceived manipulations of public communication in modern history. And the influence of the Zionist narrative upon the news media, which has effectively influenced popular Western conceptions of the Middle East conflict for nearly four decades, is more and more skillfully including fervent religious symbolism, as well as its own version of apocalyptic furor.

The third factor in our pressing concern is the conceivable horror which will accompany the fulfillment of the fundamentalist agenda. Images of a wondrous "final battle," once fantastic, are now quite reasonable. "Armageddon" has become nuclearized, and with it a violent end of history is genuinely thinkable. And such fundamentalist scenarios of the end are no longer marginal to public discourse. They have reached their way into traditional conservatism and appeared even in the places of power and influence. U.S. President Ronald Reagan has, in fact, publically revealed his fascination with the blueprint and has, on five occasions, stated that the world is headed toward an "Armageddon," or an imminent violent end (See Chapter IV, Reagan's "Armageddon Theology").

Our conclusion is that while most of the media reports have focused on the revival of fundamentalism in Islam, there has been an equally remarkable resurgence of political and theological furor among right-wing leadership in Israel, South Africa, and the United States. And it is not only in Islam that violence follows (See Chapter VIII by Goodman Smith, "They must go . . .).

The editors of the present volume see interconnections among these contemporary theopolitical expressions of fundamentalism which are not coincidental. The remarkable parallels between the situations in Palestine-Israel and South Africa suggest a connection which research confirms (See Chapters XI and XII on Apartheid Theology). Moreover, the uncritical support by Christian fundamentalists for the most expansionist actions of the Israeli government reveals a theological foundation we see as not merely inimical to justice, but hostile to world survival and peace (See Chapter I-III).

We have questioned in this volume the pretense to literate Biblical and Rabbinic interpretation by fundamentalist Zionism, whether Jewish or Christian (Chapters V and VI). We have also asked deeper questions of their theological, philosophical, and popular foundations (Chapters VII and VIII). The struggle in the Middle East has received the lion's share of our attention because of the world-destructive potential and reality of that example. We do not mean to diminish the importance of any place in which oppression and disaster may be courted in the name of the Bible. We intend to provide a telling example which demands, as is done thoughtfully and passionately by Nicholas Woltersdorff in our concluding essay, a prudent call to justice for all. Such a universalization, we hope, will help prevent false prophesy from becoming self-fulfilling.

We publish this expanded Second Edition with a word of sincere gratitude to the authors. Special thanks to Rev. Wesley Avram for his many hours of editing and colleagues at Amana Books for their guidance in the book's final form. It is our sincere hope that others will be stimulated to research and publicize their findings concerning this important subject.

Dr. Hassan Haddad
Rev. Donald E. Wagner
(Chicago, Illinois, September, 1986)

Why Christian Zionists Support Israel

BY GRACE HALSELL

In June, 1981, seated in my apartment in Washington, D.C., I listened to Israeli Prime Minister Menachem Begin being interviewed on American television. He had just ordered a strike on the Iraqi nuclear facility. The attack resulted in a few Americans questioning his use of U.S.-supplied F-16 bombers for a raid on a sovereign Arab country.

What about this criticism, he was asked.

He was not worried, he replied. Israel had *many* friends. Israel, he added, had the support of 40 million Christians.

Just previous to his television appearance, Begin, to silence any criticism of the raid on Iraq, had placed an urgent phone call for help, not to an important American rabbi, or even to an important American senator, but rather to the Rev. Jerry Falwell.

"Get to work for me," he told Falwell.

Falwell said he would—and added: "Mr. Prime Minister, I want to congratulate you for a mission that made us very proud that we manufacture those F-16s. In my opinion you must've put it right down the smokestack." ("North American Scene" *Christianity Today,* Aug. 7, 1981).

In the year that I heard Begin boast of Israel having the support of 40 million Christians, I began to research Christian Zionism. And I became convinced that Begin was right: Christian support of Israel is more important than Jewish support to the Zionist state. There may be six million American Jews who support Israel, but there are about 40 million Christians who do.

Moreover, a few Jewish Zionists from time to time will criticize Israel. And a few will even call for a Palestinian state. But no Christian Zionist will do so. They are the most loyal, the most fanatical supporters of militant Zionism. Whatever Arab lands Israel takes, a Christian Zionist will say, "They should have taken more."

I want briefly to touch on four aspects of my research on Christian Zionism. I made two trips to Palestine, under the sponsorship of Jerry Falwell. I traveled to Basel, Switzerland, to attend the first Christian Zionist Congress, and then I want to touch on what I learned at a Savannah convention late in 1985 on the scientific study of religion.

Grace Halsell, *a former White House staff writer who has written 12 books including* Journey to Jerusalem, *is the author of the forthcoming book,* On the Road to Armageddon: Crusaders for a Nuclear War, *dealing with Christian Zionism. She lives in Washington, D.C.*

(Reprinted with permission from Arab Perspectives/February-March 1986)

But first, let me say that I came to the study of Christian Zionism from a background of fundamentalism. In my case, I feel that I have been Born Again—twice. I experienced one conversion in Texas and another in Jerusalem. Let me begin with Texas.

I grew up in a small, wind-blown town on the high, dry plains of West Texas. It was said that out there one could see further—and see nothing—more so than almost anywhere.

One summer, when I was nine, I visited my maternal grandmother in Arlington, Texas, located between Dallas and Fort Worth, and in that era a dusty, quiet village of so few people that everyone knew everyone else.

A "great revivalist"—as grandmother identified a visiting preacher, otherwise known as Brother Turner—came to town, put up his tent and preached for a week. Grandmother and I attended every night. Brother Turner preached fire-and-brimstone sermons, telling us that the world is divided into the wicked and the good, and the wicked will go to hell and only those who are Born Again will escape an everlasting fire. Repent or perish, he warned.

All of us listening to him were spellbound. We had no radio, television, or public cultural events, and we depended to a great extent on the "great revivalists," such as Brother Turner, to bring us knowledge and understanding.

Each night, I experienced a sense of excited, growing anticipation. Then came the final night of the revival. Brother Turner held a large Bible in his left hand and quoted directly from God. In conclusion, he asked those who had not witnessed for Christ to come forward. Mrs. Triplett, who played the piano, then struck the notes for the well-known hymn, "Just as I am."

We stood to sing, but no one came forward. Brother Turner asked us to be seated. And he asked Mrs. Triplett to continue playing while we all bowed our heads. He asked those who knew they were saved to raise their hands and those who had not raised their hands to come forward and be saved.

Everyone seemed to be thinking of me in those moments. Everyone was softly singing. I rose from the wooden bench and moved forward, alone, to where the evangelist was standing. He welcomed me, put his arms around me, and soon my grandmother and neighbors and friends were there to embrace me.I felt myself shaking, uncontrollably. And tears were streaming down my face. I felt certain that God himself had orchestrated the holy happening.

When I was growing up, being saved was a prime topic of conversation. It was not, in our small town, considered unusual for a man, like my father, to encounter a stranger and without preliminary words of salutation ask, "Are you a Christian? Are you saved?"

What does a Fundamentalist, Born Again Christian believe? He or she generally believes the Bible is "true." That it is the word of God. And that's that. If the Bible says it, we are told, do not use your mind. Accept it as God's truth and God's will.

We had only a few books in our home, but among them we had a set of some dozen volumes called *The Book of Knowledge*. In one of these books I first saw a sketch of a dinosaur and read that scientists said the huge creatures had roamed the earth 65 million years ago. But I had been told that God created the earth 6,000 years ago. And that He did it all in only six days. And, therefore, I accepted the idea that He created dinosaurs and Adam and Eve all in the same week.

The ministers I heard all scoffed at the idea of evolution—what Darwin wrote, they insisted, was plain heresy. Once I heard the well known Texas evangelist J. Frank Norris ridicule the evolutionists by bringing apes and monkeys to his pulpit and shouting: "According to Darwin, let me introduce you to your kinfolk."

We went to church twice on Sundays. And we also went to Wednesday night prayer meetings. Generally, the Christians of my town accepted every word they found in the Bible as cardinal"truths," including:

The Jews were God's Chosen People.

And God gave the Holy Land to His Chosen People, the Jews.

And because the Jews were His Chosen People, God would bless those who blessed the Jews and curse those who cursed the Jews.

All of this was very much a part of my early indoctrination. It was, I might say, part of the air that I breathed.

Now I want to move on to my second conversion, in Jerusalem. Or at least near there. The year was 1979, and I had gone to the Holy Land without anyone knowing. I began to meet women and men of the three faiths, Christians, Muslims and Jews, who live in that land. And as part of my research for a book, I lived in the homes of families of these faiths.

I went to the portion of Palestine that is called the West Bank of the Jordan River. I talked with Palestinians who had been forced—at gun-point—to leave the land which they said their ancestors—back as long as memory served—had farmed.

I stayed in the home of a third-generation American couple, Linda and Bobby Brown, who talked about life back in the Bronx and Brooklyn. As Jews, they had immigrated to Israel, where they were issued rifles and Uzi machine guns. And, along with other recent immigrants, they confiscated land from the Palestinians to build a colony called Tekoa.

One evening, as we sat under the stars looking at the flickering lights of Arab villages, Bobby Brown said: "All the Arabs must leave this land. God gave this land to us—the Jews."

I realized in a flash the difference between the fundamentalism of my childhood and the Christian Zionism that is being preached today. In my childhood, fundamentalists argued about the age of the earth and the virgin birth of Christ. They were dealing with events in the past.

Fundamentalism changed radically with the creation of Israel. Evangelical-fundamentalists in increasing numbers began to turn to a belief system called dispensationalism. This places Israel on center stage. It says Israel must be the site for their own salvation. But, before they are saved, they must all go through seven time periods, or dispensations. The count-down history began, they tell us, with the gathering of the Jews into Palestine and the creation of Israel.

The next event, the dispensationalists tell us, will be the building of a Jewish temple.

On the 1983 tour, our group went to the Old City of Jerusalem and we approached the large Muslim grounds where the Dome of the Rock and Al-Aqsa Mosque are located. Here, too, is the Wailing Wall, where Jews gather to pray, believing the wall to be a relic from Solomon's Temple, destroyed about 2,000 years ago.

"There," said our Israeli guide, pointing to the Dome of the Rock and Al-Aqsa Mosque, "we will build our third Temple."

As we left the site, I remarked to Clyde, about 70 and a retired Minneapolis business executive, that the guide had said a temple would be built there. But, I asked, what about the Muslim shrines?

"They will be destroyed," said Clyde. "One way or another, they must be removed. You know it's in the Bible that the Temple must be rebuilt. And there's no other place for it except on that one area. You find that in the law of Moses."

Did it not seem possible, I asked Clyde, that what the Bible said about building a Temple would relate to the time in which it was written—rather than to events in the 20th century?

"No, it is related to the End Times," Clyde said. "The Bible tells us that in the End Times the Jews have renewed their animal sacrifice."

So he was convinced, I asked, that Jews, aided by Christians, should destroy the mosque, build a temple and reinstate animal sacrifices in the temple—all in order to please God?

That, said Clyde, was the way it had to be. It was in the Bible.

Many Christians who feel the same way have formed the Temple Mount Foundation to help remove the Muslim shrines. I have talked with several leaders of the Temple Mount Foundation. Several are wealthy. They are not ashamed of their plans to destroy the Dome of the Rock and Al-Aqsa Mosque.

The Reverend James DeLoach of Houston's Second Baptist Church visited me in Washington, D.C., and told me that he and others in the Temple Mount Foundation had raised and spent tens of thousand of dollars to defend Israelis charged with assaults on the mosques.

What, I asked, if the Israelis they support are successful? And they destroy the mosques. And this triggers World War III and a nuclear holocaust—would he and his colleagues not be responsible?

We hear, in this country, a great deal about Shiite fanatics who go on suicidal missions because they believe they are doing the will of God. We hear much less about Christians who are millionaires, dress in fine suits and look like our brothers or our uncles. They do not look like the stereotype fanatic. Yet they believe if they start a nuclear war, they are doing God's will.

Far from working to make peace, all dispensationalists believe that it is God's will, indeed, His command, that we fight a nuclear Armageddon.

On the 1983 trip, our group traveled to the valley of Megiddo, located about an hour's drive north of Tel Aviv. As we left the bus, my steps again fell in with Clyde's, the retired Minneapolis businessman.

"At last!" Clyde remarked, as we looked out over the valley, "I am viewing the site of Armageddon!"

Then he explained that a 200-million-man army will invade Israel, and the last, great decisive battle will involve all the armies of the earth, and this battle—involving nuclear weapons, would kill most of the earth's inhabitants.

But Clyde—along with Jerry Falwell and other Born Again Christians—do not expect to be here for this nuclear holocaust. They say they will be Raptured—lifted up in the clouds—just before it all begins. With this escape hatch, Clyde said he actually looked forward to the End of Time.

Early in 1985, I signed to go on another Falwell-sponsored tour—and again I received a colored brochure of the trip, printed in Israel. Although we would be 850 Christians traveling to the Land of Christ, Falwell in his brochure made not a single mention of Christ.

Once we arrived, we had only Israeli Jewish guides. We had no Christian guide—to any of the sites where Christ was born, died or had his ministry.

I had a list of several American Christians living in Nazareth, and I asked our Israeli guide if our group might have time to meet them.

"No," he said, "The bus will not stop in Nazareth."

No one contested the guide's decision. On the outskirts of Nazareth, however, our Israeli guide changed his mind.

"We will stop in Nazareth for 20 minutes," he announced, "to use the toilet facilities."

And thus we stopped. And we left Nazareth, without having seen it.

We proceeded to Jerusalem, where Falwell chose to honor Ariel Sharon. All 850 of us gathered for the occasion. In introducing Sharon, Falwell said that in the annals of history, only a few great men came along. He named George Washington, Abraham Lincoln—and Ariel Sharon!

As the burly former general spoke, saying America made a mistake in stopping the slaughter of Palestinians and Lebanese in the battle of Beirut, the Christians rose repeatedly to their feet in applause.

In 1983, Falwell had honored then defense minister Moshe Arens. Arens praised the Israeli invasion of Lebanon—which killed and wounded tens of thousand of Palestinians and Lebanese, most of them civilians, and said the United States should back Israel in future wars—"to wipe out the enemies." As Falwell spoke, the Christians jumped to their feet, applauding and shouting "Amen" and "Hallelujah!"

In late August of 1985 I went to Basel, Switzerland, to attend the first Christian Zionist Congress. I was one of 589 persons from 27 countries attending this congress—held in the same hall where Theodor Herzl convened the first Jewish Zionist Congress—88 years ago.

For three days I listened to Christian speakers review the horrors of the holocaust. No speaker, Jew or Christian, suggested that somehow all humankind must, in a nuclear age, learn to live as good neighbors.

Rather than provide hope by suggesting steps whereby Jews and Arabs might reach reconciliation and peace, each speaker seemed to reinforce the Jews' haunting fears about security. Rather than stressing how much Arabs and Jews and, indeed, all human beings have in common, speakers told us: Jews are different. They must live exclusively among Jews.

The Christians proposed a resolution urging Israel to annex the West Bank, with its near one million Palestinians. An Israeli Jew, seated in the audience, rose—before the motion was voted upon—to suggest that the language be modified. He pointed out that an Israeli poll showed that one third of the Israelis would be willing to trade territory seized in 1967 for peace with the Palestinians.

In answer to that, one Christian leader shouted: "We don't care what the Israelis vote! We care what God says! And God gave the land to the Jews!"

The Christians then passed the resolution.

In conclusion, I want to report what I learned at a recent conference in Savannah, Georgia, on the scientific study of religion.

At this meeting I heard results of a Nielsen survey on TV evangelists. It reveals that 40 per cent of all U.S. families that have television sets watch TV evangelists at least once a month. All major TV evanglists—with only one exception—are Christian Zionists. This means that 45 million Americans regularly listen to dispensationalists who make a cult of Israel.

Here's a breakdown of the popularity of the TV evangelists:

Pat Robertson, who hosts the daily 700 Club, reaches more than 16 million households. That's slightly more than 19 per cent of all Americans.

Jimmy Swaggart reaches a total of 4.5 million households daily and a total of 9.2 million households on Sundays.

Jim Bakker is watched by nearly 5 million households daily.

Oral Roberts, nearly 6 million households weekly.

Jerry Falwell, more than 5 million households weekly.

Kenneth Copeland, nearly 5 million households weekly.

Rex Humbard, about 4 million households weekly.

All of these TV evangelists are Christian Zionists. They all put Israel on center stage. They endorse whatever Israel does.

Today, it seems, American Christians are largely in two groups: the first group, with about 40 million people, makes a cult of Israel. And as part of this cult, they say that in any war with Israel, God always fights on the side of the Israelis.

The second group includes all the other Christians who do not criticize the cult of Israel for fear someone will say—"What, have you forgotten the holocaust!" Or, "You are anti-Semitic."

The task of educating the Christians on Middle East issues—and, I will add, Christ's true mission of peace—is a large one. Statistics tell us that an increasingly large number of Americans are tuning in to TV evangelists who preach a dispensationalist—or cult of Israel—theology. And they are pushing us steadily toward a nuclear Armageddon.

The Cult of Israel and Palestinian Human Rights

BY HASSAN HADDAD

"Palestinians have human rights too" goes the slogan of the Palestine Human Rights Campaign (PHRC). The fact that such a statement which should go without saying, has to be made, is not only a reflection on the violation of these rights by Israel, but a finger of accusation pointed at supporters of Israel everywhere. The fact that PHRC has had to bring this message to the American people and struggle to create an awareness of the simple truth that the Palestinians are also entitled to a full measure of humanity compels us to investigate the causes of this moral myopia. Confronted with another odd reality, namely that many of those who turn a deaf ear to the plight of the Palestinians do so partially or totally because of religious conviction based primarily on improper and selective reading of the Bible, especially the Old Testament, the investigation of the roots of this bias becomes a serious matter, indeed a ministry.

The use and abuse of the Bible in reflecting on the legitimacy, policies, and conduct of Israel is so common, especially, but not exclusively, among American conservative Christians. This unfortunate linkage between Biblical Israel and the modern Jewish State is not restricted to religious Zionists and Christian fundamentalists. It is quite common, and more dangerously so, among the general public, whose knowledge of the Bible is restricted and whose biblicism is as strong as it is uncritical. Most Christians are reminded constantly since childhood of the uniqueness and holiness of Biblical Israel and of its distinction beyond human and moral considerations. Once a linkage between Biblical Israel and the modern state is established, this suprahuman quality of Biblical Israel is unconsciously, or with intent, transferred to modern Israel. The common belief in the historical relevance of the Bible in its entirety to the present and the future adds a measure of predestinate status to the State of Israel and its sacred centrality in current and future history.

There are supporters and advocates of Israel who have either been blind to the tragedy of the Palestinians, or have openly and knowingly preached their elimination. And then there are those who are aware of the injustice done to the Palestinians by the creation of Israel in Palestine, but seek to see this injustice only in the context of what they consider to be compelling Biblical imperatives. "God's ways," clearly deliniated in the scriptures for Israel's apologists, cannot be questioned by the merely human. To them Israel, in spite of its shortcomings, is the focal point of God's Plan as revealed in the Bible. The violence that accompanied the creation of the Jewish State and the course of its short history is also Biblical. Armageddon, the ultimate universal massacre, is the necessary God-ordained outcome of the sinister conspiracy by the Evil Empire and its allies to wage war on Israel. To them the Biblical prophecies seem to be quite clear and specific on this issue.

The history of condoning evil in the name of the Bible is a long one. Evils of discrimination, oppression, and war are justified by reference to texts in the Bible, in most cases out of historical context. The Crusaders and all the violent religious wars, the abuse of authority, slavery, discrimination against other races, other cultures, other gods, were done in the name of the Bible. The near extermination of the Amerindians had Biblical backing. Until recently racial discrimination in America was justified by Biblical text. Dispossessing and expelling the Palestinians to make room for a Zionist Jewish State is amply represented by parallels, or by prophecies in the Bible. The disenfranchisement of Blacks in South Africa's Apartheid ystem is done according to some tenuous readings in the Old Testament.[1] All this and more, even today, is done in the name of the Bible, and quite often condoned and encouraged by those who are religious persons: ministers, priests, and rabbis who should know the other side of the scripture, the one that deals with love, equality, forgiveness, and with the universal compassion of a universal God.

In the hands of those who are totally committed to Israel on religious grounds (and consequently display total disregard for the legitimate rights of the Palestinians), the Bible seems to have turned from an instrument inspiring love and compassion to one inciting discrimination and vengeance. The brand of biblicism that comes through in the publications of the far Christian right (such as Hal Lindsay's *The Late Great Planet Earth)* and scores of like minded publications, by the sermons of many of the preachers of the electronic church (such as Jimmy Swaggart, Jerry Falwell, and Mike Evans, to mention but a few) has focused the attention of the flock on the State of Israel as a very central and essential component of the Christian faith, and helped consequently, in blocking any human, moral, or theological consideration of the injustice done to a whole people at the hands of Israel.

This trend has been growing steadily in America, especially since 1967 when Israel conquered Jerusalem and, in doing so confirmed further, according to the fundamentalists, the veracity of the Biblical prophecies.[2] This preoccupation with Biblical prophecy keeps plaguing the Christian churches, especially in this electronic era, diverting the attention of the preachers and their faithful flocks from Jesus' message of universal love and fellowship to that part of the Bible which deals with the political and the eschatological destiny of Israel. From this preoccupation with Israel as the center of God's plan for human history, a "Cult of Israel" has emerged.

The cult of Israel promotes Armageddon at the expense of Bethlehem. The gospel, with its good news of the universal love of God, takes second place to the books of the Old Testament where violence in the service of the tribes of Israel is not only permitted but often recommended. The Sermons and the parables of Jesus of Nazareth that emphasize the human condition within the universal patrimony of God are eclipsed by the strong and menacing words of the prophetic books of Ezekiel, Daniel, and John's apocalypse. The wrath of God becomes paramount and His love reserved only for one chosen entity.

The cult of Israel, with strong roots in the Old Testament, predates the establishment of the Jewish state in Palestine. In fact, the cult is the basis on which the Zionist movement is built and on which Christian Zionism has developed. It accounts for most of the pro-Israel sentiments in the Western-Christian world, especially since the Balfour Declaration of 1917. It helps explain the American anxious commitment to recognize Israel in 1948, even before the ceremony which declared its existence was concluded, and to give Israel total support even at the cost of American national and international interests. No mere political, economic, or diplomatic conditions can totally explain the "moral," financial, and military support that the United States has been giving to Israel in spite of the many flagrant breaches by Israel of this American trust.

The cult of Israel gives the present-day Jewish state a special status that goes beyond that of a foreign political entity that would normally be dealt with through the channels of diplomacy and would be subject to the dictates of international law.

The cultic dimension of American infatuation with Israel can best explain the enigmatic "special relationship," the "moral commitment," and the incomparable economic and military umbilical cord between the U.S. and Israel. According to the pundits of the cult, American aid to Israel is very necessary, not only for the survival of the Jewish State, but for the well-being, even the survival, of the United States of America. This is so, because God will preserve any nation that helps Israel and will punish those who oppose it. This unusual assumption is based on a Biblical text that has become the cornerstone of the cult. The Book of Genesis states that God said to Abraham, "I will bless those who bless thee and curse those who curse thee."[3] This little bit of personal history, thousands of years old, has, by some magical feat of transference, become the article of faith for those who make the state of Israel the cornerstone of their religious and historical outlook. Moreover, it also became, in a bizarre way, the justification for the oppression of the Palestinians whose destiny, like that of Israel, has been divinely preordained, again by textual manipulation of the Bible. The Palestinians, like the Canaanites who confronted Biblical Israel, had to be eliminated, not primarily for political reasons, not because there was no room in the land, but because they "polluted the land." Their isolation, even elimination is ordered by the Lord Himself.[4]

The cult of Israel has two sides to it. On one side we find a total and irrational support of Israel and, on the other, an equally irrational disregard of the Palestinians, their rights, their humanity, their persons. These two elements of the problem are closley interrelated, and cannot be easily and successfully discussed separately. While the blessing to Abraham mentioned above is reserved for the Jews, the curse is likewise a divine order of condemnation for the Palestinians who, by claiming their birthright in the land of Palestine, have incurred the wrath of God and the hatred of the "faithful."

It could be argued that the disregard of Palestinian legitimate rights in the West is a product of a long cultural and historical bias against Arabs and Muslims in general. But the cult of Israel adds another dimension to this bias. It intensifies it beyond its cultural and historical dimensions into an uncompromising rejection rooted in religious conviction. While the Palestinians are sometimes denounced by the secular supporters of Israel for opposing what they consider a humanitarian and democratic institution, its "religious" proponents seem to regard the Palestinians as the anti-Christ for obstructing the fulfillment of God's plans and retarding the Second Coming. The term "terrorists" applied indiscriminately to all Palestinians, regardless of the nature of their activities in asserting their fundamental rights, is a product of this pro-Israel cultic mentality.

The cult of Israel has prevented its adherents from seeing the Palestinians in their own terms. This is only the cultic-religious side of a denial of their humanity that was also expressed in economic and even biological terms. The Palestinians were thus not only deprived by the Jewish settlers in Palestine (and by all those who concurred with them and encouraged them) of the inherent human right to have one's own culture understood and respected, but they were also ruthlessly deprived of land and livelihood and all too often of life itself. This is the primal crime attached to the cult of Israel, and it touches not only the settlers on the land, but their supporters in the West. We must ask what in the hearts of the Jews and of the Christians of the West kept so many for so long from seeing any crime at all in this venture.[5]

Modern Israel, in this cult, is claimed as a direct descendant of the Biblical Israel, as a continuation and fulfillment of an historical entity based on a divine election and a sacred promise of land. Accordingly, the chosen do not have to justify their favored position on humanitarian and moral grounds, or apologize for their disregard for the rights of others. Their position is predetermined by a divine order. The primal crime, if its existence is admitted at all, is not of their doing. The task of creating a purely Jewish state in Palestine is of such historical magnitude, and such divine concept, that the dispossession of the Palestinians, no matter how "regretful," dims into insignificance in proportion.[6]

A narrow and literal reading of the scriptures, a common practice among many Jews and many more Christians, makes the destiny of Israel and that of the Palestinians a mutually exclusive matter. Thus, the removal of the Palestinians from the land which is reserved by divine order for the chosen people, is essential for the purity, welfare, and security of the Jewish State, and as such, a part of the divine plan. One party had to disappear to make room for the other, not for the lack of room, not because they could not live together, but because they should not live together. Thus the decision to remove the Palestinians and to deny them their fundamental rights was not motivated only by political, economic, or social considerations, but by an added dimension of religious, mystical conviction, one that, by its nature, is unreasonable and uncompromising. Its total dogmatism is placed at the doorstep of the Lord Himself.

To admit that Palestinians have rights in the land of their birth—to some even admitting that they do exist at all—is one way of denying or questioning this exclusive divine patrimony. Hence, the refusal of every Israeli government on the right or on the left of the political spectrum, to recognize the Palestinians, let alone the PLO, cannot be explained only in terms of political advantage or political expediency. There is a Biblical, cultic conviction behind it. American concurrence with that position is likewise attributable in part to the same Biblical basis.

On the American and Western side, the Biblical anchor of pro-Israeli sentiment justifies Israel's actions in claiming Arab territories and in striking at the Palestinians for asserting their right to these territories. This attitude reflects a commitment of faith, as some theologians would have it, even those representing mainline churches.[7] To raise questions about such commitments amounts to heresy to some conservative churchmen. For, if one accepts the principle of the divinely favored person, one is only a short step away from accepting the principle of the divinely cursed and dispossessed person.

The territorial dimension of the cult of Israel claims the exclusive right to the Holy Land (Palestine) for the exclusively chosen holy race. David Ben-Gurion called the Bible the "sacrosanct title-deed to Palestine" for the Jewish People.[8] Zionism in fact, and by strong implication of the name itself, puts the "territorial imperative" exclusively in Palestine. This is basically a Biblical imperative. The Biblical "promise" is clearly a promise of the Land of Canaan (Palestine). No substitute land could be acceptable to the vast majority of Zionists. This has become a conviction that needs no explanation to most Jews and conservative Christians. Even "liberal" Zionists, such as Martin Buber, have a mystical attachment to that particular piece of land as the "Land of Promise." "For the Bible tells us," he wrote to Gandhi, "[that our way of life] cannot be realized by individuals in the sphere of their private existence, but only a nation in the establishment of its society [in a] communal ownership of the land (Leveticus 25:23)."[9] This apotheosis of the "Land of Israel" linked mystically to that of the "People Israel," is the essential ingredient in religious Zionism. The Land of Palestine was created by the Almighty and consecrated since creation to accomodate the Chosen People. This is a non-negotiable right, according to Jewish and Christian Zionists, all in the name of the Bible.

Given this "mystery" in the connection between the Jews and the land of Palestine, the right of the Jews, on one side, and the denial of that of the Palestinians on the other, are both made absolute. The ultra-conservative Christian takes this road without any apologies. The ultra-nationalist Zionists, such as Rabbi Meir Kahane and many other Rabbis who are not as vociferous, but equally committed to the cult of the Land of Israel, also stand by their religious convictions in demanding exclusive Jewish right to Palestine.[10] But many so-called liberal Zionists, as well as some mainline Christian churches and theologians, have worked diligently to produce an apologetic system of justification for the Jewish claim to Palestine without having to appear insensitive to the suffering of Palestinians.[11] Martin Buber's *Brit Shalom* (covenant of peace) preaches the coexistence between Jews and Arabs in Palestine. But his Biblical and Talmudic alter-ego insists on the holiness of the connection between the Jews and Palestine, thus excluding an honest and equal sharing of Palestine by Jews and non-Jews. His attitude towards the Palestinians is one of condescending tolerance at best, not of equality in the sight of God. Buber seems to be saying "Palestinians have human rights too," but in his writings on Israel he asserts the divine right of the Jews to Palestine. A divine right certainly outweighs a human one in his opinion and that of Christian Zionists.

Many "liberal" Zionists, are devotees of the Cult of Israel. They elevate the question of Israel, the people, and the land to the level of the divine. They worship the Golden Calf while claiming the universality of God. Reform Rabbi Eugene Borowitz asserted after the six day war in June 1967 that the concern "throughout the Jewish world"

> . . . was not military—who should win. It was theological. Would God abandon the people of Israel again and allow the citizens of the State of Israel to be slaughtered by Arab armies? . . . It was not, then, only the Israeli armies who were on trial that day but, in very earnest, God himself.[12]

Buber's cult of Israel, especially as the Promised Land, seems to have reached an extreme form of fetishism. "The world can be redeemed only by the redemption of Israel and Israel can be redeemed only by re-union with its land."[13] "Like the Torah and the sanctuary, the Land of Israel is also part of the original Creation.[14] This marriage between the People Israel and the Land at the hand of the Almighty God makes this holy piece of earth worthy only of the holy race. This leaves Buber's "humanism" towards the Arabs in great doubt. Paraphrasing statements by Rabbi Liva and Maimonides, he writes: "God has planted this people neither with the left hand nor with his right hand but with both hands; it is his own people. And so this people and this land belong together from the beginning, by reason of their very nature."[15]

The increasing preoccupation of the fundamentalist Christians with the Biblical text dealing with Israel's history and its prophetic future keeps the State of Israel on their minds and in their sermons. Most Christians, therefore, cannot escape confronting the issue of the relevance of the State of Israel to their beliefs, hence taking a stand, mostly a negative one, toward Palestinian human rights. Rejecting any relevance of the question of Israel to their religious life might require some difficult revision of beliefs installed since childhood and some strenuous theological exercises. Accepting it, on the other hand, is accepting on faith the total and absolute authority of the Biblical text. Either way, Israel is a question of concern to most American Christians. Their awareness of the Jewish State, its problems, wars, and enemies exceed their awareness of any other country.

Most fundamentalists support Israel wholeheartedly because they believe that the creation of the Jewish State is a sign, according to Biblical prophecies, that the Messiah is coming. To them the Jew, in his present state of non-belief, may not be totally an acceptable person. But he is still a chosen one who will eventually be saved. No such status is accorded to any one else, especially the Palestinians. They are hopelessly locked into a negative role. They are non-persons, and non-persons have no claim to rights. Their greatest misfortune is that they constitute a stumbling block in the road of "salvation." The term "terrorist" usually and eagerly given to Palestinians takes on an added meaning. It contains eternal evil connotations: an evil that is as predestined and absolute as the chosenness of the holy race and the salvation of the true believers are predestined and absolute.

The cult of Israel, with its total and unqualified approval of the Jewish state, and its damnation of its enemies finds perfect expression in an advertisement placed by a large group of churchmen in 1976. It says in part:

> Because the Jewish people are the people of prophecy they are the people of the land. And we, knowing Him who made the promise, totally support the people and the land of Israel in her God-given, God-promised, God-

> ordained right to exist. Any person or group of nations opposed to this right isn't just fighting Israel. But God and Time itself.[16]

According to this statement of cult, Israel is the only nation in the world established by divine order. God's wrath will fall on any person or nation that dares to oppose it.

How, one might ask, can the Palestinian Arabs claim any right, compassion or justice, when they are fighting not only Israel, but God, and Time itself?!

NOTES

1. White Afrikaaner nationalists claim that their control of South Africa is a covenant with God, similar to the Old Testament covenant with Israel. The Blacks are the Canaanites, not only symbolically, but racially, since the Old Testament makes them the descendants of Ham who is the father of all blacks. According to the Biblical legend, Ham had a curse put on him by his father Noah when the old man was seen naked by his son. This curse applies to all the descendants of Ham, Canaanites especially (predecessors of the modern Palestinians), and all blacks, whose blackness and enslavement are the deserved outcome of that curse. The story of the curse on Ham and Canaan is in Genesis 9:20-28. The essential verses are: "Cursed be Canaan; a slave of slaves shall he be to his brothers," and "Blessed by the lord my God be Shem; and let Canaan be his slave." This text was also used to justify slavery in America and elsewhere. A rabbinical commentator on this curse maintains that "Canaan, in a certain sense, was predestined to this and similar offenses; for he was begotten by his father while in Noah's Ark, whereas God had commanded that the sexes shuld live separately therein (Gen. xxxvi), (The Jewish Encyclopedia, article: Canaan).

2. On the subject of Biblical prophecy, a good analysis of the misuse of the scriptures for predicting future events is Dewey M. Beagle, *Prophecy and Prediction,* Pryor Petengill, Ann Arbor, MI, 1978.

3. Genesis 12:3. This verse is used by some opponents of Zionism also. They point out that God's blessing on Abraham covers both of his sons, Ishmael and Isaac. The Arabs, who are supposedly the descendants of Ishmael, are also included in the blessing. This argument "enlarges" the circle of the blessed, but does not reject the discriminatory divine choice on the basis of race.

4. Biblical texts used to promote the prohibition of mixing and intermarriage with the people of the land are many. See especially the Book of Deuteronomy (e.g. chapter 7), and Ezra 9:10-15. For the final solution to the problem of the Gentiles of the Land by killing them off, the most representative text is in Deuteronomy 7:1-5 stating in part, "When the Lord your God gives them over to you, and you defeat them; then you must utterly destroy them; you shall make no covenant with them, and show no mercy to them . . . "

5. On this subject of the primal crime as applied to the treatment of the Native American by the "New Israelites" see Robert Bella, *The Broken Covenant,* New York, The Seabury Press, 1975.

6. A typical statement about the primacy of Israel over all considerations was made by Rabbi Nissim, chief Rabbi of Israel in 1968: "The Land of Israel was, with its borders, defined for us by Divine Providence. Thou shall be said the Almighty, and there it is; no power on earth can alter that which was created by Him. In this connection it is not a question of law or logic; neither is it a matter of human treatment or that sort of thing." in *Hayom* June 7, 1968. Rabbi Meir Kahane, in his book *They Must Go,* (Grosset & Dunlap, New York, 1981) makes that same point a basis of his work, with ample references to Biblical, Talmudic, and Rabbinical texts. See also note 8, below.

7. See, for example, Lutheran theologian Richard John Neuhaus, *Christian Faith and Public Policy,* (Minneapolis: Augsburg Publishing House, 1977, with statements such as: "The U.S. has a single responsibility to Israel . . . The steadfastness and dependability of U.S. commitment to Israel's survival as a state must never be permitted to be thrown into question . . . This thinking about Israel is singularly affected by the relationship between living Judaism and the Church, a relationship which remains a great mystery and is marked by a much tortured history. In this relationship God has exercised judgment beginning with the house of faith" (p. 90). Reinhold Niebuhr, one of the most influential American theologians of the 20th century was a great champion of Zionism and of Israel, primarily on theological grounds. For a more detailed treatment of this subject see H.S. Haddad, "Christian Zionism in America: The Religious Factor in American Middle East Policy," in Bashir K. Nijim, ed., *American Church Politics and the Middle East,* AAUG Publications, Belmont, MA, 1982, pp. 109-133.

8. David Ben-Gurion, *The Rebirth and Destiny of Israel,* New York, Philosophical Library, 1954, p. 100.

9. Martin Buber, *Israel and the World: Essays in a Time of Crisis,* Schocken Books, New York, 1948, p. 229. In his letter to Gandhi, who had accused the Zionists of land grabbing, Buber makes sweeping statements about the holiness of the land: " . . . the question of our Jewish destiny is indissolubly bound up with the possibility of ingathering, and that is bound up with Palestine." (p.227). Buber's conditions for the "Chosen Nation" based on Biblical texts, makes this communal ownership of the land of Palestine a top priority. "We could not and cannot renounce the Jewish claim;" he adds, "something even higher than the life of our people is bound up with this land, namely its work, its divine mission." (p.231).

10. See article by Goodman Smith in this volume on Meir Kahane's views on Jewish nationalism and the Arabs in Israel.

11. Neuhaus (note 7 above) recognizes the injustice done to the Palestinians and admits that the Churches should be sensitive to their plight. But he goes on from there to assert the right of the Jews to Palestine. This is a typical attitude of the "liberal" churches—to admit the injustice but, because of the influence of their traditional Biblical world-view, to profess total helplessness in advocating openly the rights of the Palestinian people to home and country. Reinhold Niebuhr went further to suggest that the Palestinian refugees should be compensated and resettled in other Arab land, but not return to their homes in Palestine (quoted in Herzel Fishman, *American Protestantism and a Jewish State,* Detroit, Wayne State University Press, 1973, p. 74).

12. Rabbi Eugene B. Borowitz, "Hope Jewish and Hope Secular," in *The Future as the Presence of Shared Hope,* ed. by M. Muckenhirn, Sheed and Ward, New York, 1968, p. 107.

13. Martin Buber, *On Zion: The History of an Idea,* Schocken Books, New York, 1973, p. 77.

14. *Ibid.*, p. 48.

15. *Ibid.*, p. 87.

16. Chicago Tribune, July 1, 1976.

Anxious for Armageddon: Probing Israel's Political Support Among American Fundamentalists

BY DONALD E. WAGNER

Most students of the Palestinian-Israeli conflict are unaware of the crucial political role that Christian fundamentalists have played to facilitate the goals of the maximalist wing ("all of Palestine is Jewish") in the Zionist movement. It is not widely known, for example, that the early catch-phrase of the Zionists — "a land of no people for a people with no land" — was coined by a Christian fundamentalist nearly sixty years before Theodore Herzl employed it.

Or how many people realize that the first major lobby effort in the United States on behalf of the Jewish state occurred as early as 1891? The campaign was conceived and choreographed by the Christian fundamentalist author and preacher, William Blackstone. A few years later, when Herzl wavered in his commitment to Palestine as the potential site of the Jewish state, Blackstone sent him a marked copy of the Old Testament in order to reinforce his conviction that Jews must return only to the Holy Land in order to fulfill Bible prophecy.[1] The marked Bible is displayed today near Herzl's tomb in Jerusalem.

Palestinians and their advocates should not be surprised by the current groundswell of support that Israel receives in the United States from Christian fundamentalists. Nor is it unique for an American President, Pentagon officials, and key Senators or Congresspersons to become enchanted with Christian Zionist themes such as "Armageddon." The Reagan Administration is not the first team to employ such rhetoric, nor will they be the last. However, what is surprising is the fact that Middle East analysts and progressive forces continue to underestimate the political power of fundamentalist Christian Zionists.

Christian fundamentalist support of Revisionist Zionism has a long and complicated history, perhaps too extensive to summarize in this brief essay. Therefore, the following study will examine the essential doctrines of one aspect of Christian Zionism, the American fundamentalists. It will summarize the historical developments which gave rise to fundamentalist Christian Zionism and then highlight representative leaders and the organizations that are functioning in the United States today. It will become clear that Christian fundamentalists predated Revisionist Zionism and paved the way for both popular and political support of its ideology even at the highest levels in Western governments.

What Do Fundamentalist Christian Zionists Believe?

Christian Zionism takes numerous forms today ranging from the highly visible fundamentalist preacher Rev. Jerry Falwell to the liberal Catholic and former Congressman Fr. Robert Drinan. Our particular focus in this study is the fundamentalist understanding of Christian Zionism, which we will define as:

> The belief that the return of the Jews to Palestine and creation of a modern and exclusively Jewish state, Israel, are the fulfillment of Biblical prophecy. Additional signs indicate that history has entered its last stage, which will include the final battle with the Anti-Christ at Armageddon and the Second Coming of Jesus Christ.

At the outset of the study it will be wise to clarify a common misconception concerning the terms evangelical and fundamentalist. The Greek root word for evangelical ("euangellion") means "one who shares the good news," meaning the Gospel of Jesus Christ. The contemporary connotation of the term evangelical, as utilized in the secular media, today encompasses over 50 million Americans, ranging from the televangelists (Jimmy Swaggart, Pat Robertson), Dr. Billy Graham, and the radical Sojourners Community. Dr. Graham would be representative of mainstream evangelical Christianity, the majority of whom do not subscribe to the above position. The evangelical "left," such as Sojourners, is an increasingly influential but numerically small segment of evangelicalism. They support a progressive political agenda on peace and human rights concerns. Very few, if any, from the "left" would support the fundamentalist's political positions.

However, the most visible and fastest growing branch within the evangelical movement is fundamentalism, or the "Evangelical Right." They can be subdivided into two communities. First, the traditional fundamentalists, whose roots date back to 1885-1920 era when numerous doctrinal battles raged over evolution, scientific analysis, and "modernism." Their name was derived from a series of pamphlets issued between 1910-1915 titled "The Fundamentals". Such spokesmen as William Jennings Bryan and Princeton theologian James Gresham Machen sought to defend the faith against the satanic influences of liberalism. According to "The Fundamentals", the irreducible doctrines are: the deity of Jesus Christ, the Virgin Birth, the bodily Resurrection, substitutionary atonement through Christ, the imminent Second Coming of Jesus, and most important, the primacy of the Bible as God's inerrant word. Many fundamentalists withdrew into an apolitical stance and formed a subculture into themselves after the Scopes' trial and similar public setbacks following World War I.

The other tradition within the evangelical "right" has roots as far back as the Protestant Reformation but has only recently become a massive movement. This second tradition of fundamentalism combines many of the above mentioned doctrines but heightens the accent on eschatology. They are the premillennialists, who believe that Jesus will return to earth very soon to establish a thousand year rule of peace ("Millennium"). After the "final judgment", people will be doomed for eternity or enter Paradise. The apocalyptic book of Revelation, particularly chapter 20:1-6, is an important Biblical basis for this view.

The premillennialists teach that the world will continue to degenerate whereas evil and the rule of the Anti-Christ will gain control, necessitating a final battle at Armageddon (the plain of Megiddo in Israel) and the return of Jesus. Of more significance than the Christian Church, according to premillennialist doctrine, is the central role to be played by Israel during the final phase of history. It is Israel that will rise as a military power and defeat the Northern satanic force (interpreted as the Soviet Union) prior to Jesus' Second Coming (see Ezekiel 38-39). Jesus will then return to establish a thousand year reign of peace.

The fixation upon Israel as a literal fulfillment of Biblical prophecy and the priority it is given within the premillennialist theological system has become a major source of support for the Jewish state. Today the multi-million dollar televangelists, the vast majority of whom are premillennialists, have established a symbiotic relationship with Israel's political leadership and must now be seen as having major influence on President Reagan, the Pentagon, and U.S. foreign policy.

Historical Perspectives

American fundamentalism adopted the Revisionist Zionist agenda completely independent of pressure or contacts with Jewish Zionists. The major source of Christian Zionist doctrine gaining a foothold in the United States was British fundamentalism, where an identification with Israel had developed over fifteen centuries.

Pulitzer Prize winning historian Barbara Tuchman, while herself a Zionist, attributes the British attachment to "Israel" to two factors: first, a literal interpretation of the Bible and its translation into English; second, England's colonial need for a landbridge to India and her subsequent desire to secure Middle East oil. Tuchman examines these and other historical dynamics in her important volume *Bible and Sword,* elaborating upon the development of literary, cultural and religious symbolism which depicted England as the "New Israel" (similar use of the "New Israel" concept are still alive in South Africa, the United States, and the Israeli settlement movement — see Chapters V — VIII).

As Tuchman develops these and related arguments, she explores the literary, cultural, political and religious symbolism which were created to undergrid England's imperial aspirations. Clearly, the British saw themselves as God's chosen vessels and at an early phase of English history, the Biblical symbols, popular writings and identification with Biblical Israel united the British with the Jewish people.

Tuchman cites the earliest known essay in English literature, the "Epistle of Gildas" (written about 550 A.D.), which employs analogies from the Old Testament to depict England's struggle for survival. In this case, England was compared to Israel who defeated the hated Philistines in order to become a people of destiny.[3] Similar analogies were utilized by England's literary giants, such as the Venerable Bede (ninth century), John Milton, William Wordsworth, George Eliot, and many others.

What Tuchman failed to observe due to her uncritical bias toward Zionism one finds corrected in a new study by Regina Sharif. Her survey of three centuries of western history focuses exclusively upon Gentile contributions to Zionism. Sharif traces the roots of modern Gentile Zionism to the Protestant Reformation and the Puritan Revolution. She attributes the Reformer's principles of "the priesthood of all believers", of placing the Bible in the hands of the people, and the tendency toward biblical literalism as responsible for a dramatic shift in Western Christendom. In addition, the Puritan's preoccupation with Old Testament themes combined with Europe's lust for the Holy Land (leftover from the Crusades) and contributed to the rise of Christian Zionism.

Perhaps the earliest British theologian to advocate Jewish "restoration" in Palestine (which is the essence of Zionism) was Rev. Thomas Brightman (1585). While his publications received little public attention during the Elizabethan literary renaissance, one of Brightman's students, Sir Henry Finch, became a member of Parliament and developed a large following. In 1621, Finch wrote the following:

> (The Jews) shall repair to their own country — shall inhabit all the parts of the land as before, (they) shall live in safety, and shall continue in it forever.[4]

Despite these early pioneers, Christian Zionism was neither systematized nor truly popular among the masses until after the French Revolution. As had been the case throughout history, millennarian thought emerged during periods of great social and economic upheaval. Immediately following the American and French Revolutions, traditional interpretations of history and life in general were called into question and the British turned to a heightened awareness of God's impending judgement. Historian LeRoy Froom summarized the period:

> After the troublous times of the American Revolution and its aftermath, and especially after the devastating effects of the infidelic French philosophy, men turned again to the Bible for light, especially the prophecies of Daniel and Revelation. They were seeking a satisfying explanation of the prevailing irreligion of the time and to find God's way out of the situation.[5]

Not everyone turned to their Bibles for comfort and direction, but many did. Theologians and the clergy began to revive their favorite Apocalyptic passages which were increasingly interpreted to provide clues to God's future plans for history. At the same time, these passages took on a literal focus concerning Israel and the return of the Jews to Palestine.

One of the important spokesmen for Christian Zionism during this period was an Anglican clergyman named Rev. Louis Way. After studying Bible prophecy and developing a fascination with Jewish restoration in Palestine, Way became (in 1809) director of a floundering missionary group, the London Society for Promoting Christianity among the Jews. Through his efforts, the Society became a powerful force, largely through its popular journal, *The Jewish Expositor.*

Way emphasized three key elements in his approach to Christian Zionism: "restoration" of the Jews in Palestine as a fulfillment of Biblical prophecy; careful charting of contemporary events which indicate that Jesus' return is near; a restored Jewish state should make no provision for the Arabs and must be envisioned as exclusively Jewish. Rev. Way's teachings had an enormous effect upon several M.P.'s, many academics and writers such as Samuel Taylor Coleridge, who was a devout follower of Way.[6]

The second influential figure during this period was the Honorable Henry Drummond, a member of the British House of Commons for more than a decade. Ernest Sandeen, a historian of this period, has noted that Drummond's famed Albury Conferences (named after his estate) more than any other event, gave structure to the British millenarian revival, consolidating both the theology and the group of men who were to defend it. The Conference in 1829, for example, issued the following outline of their doctrine:

> 1. This 'dispensation' or age will not end insensibly but cataclysmically in judgement and destruction of the church in the same manner in which the Jewish dispensation ended; 2. The Jews will be restored in Palestine during the time of judgement; 3. The judgement to come will fall principally upon Christendom; 4. When the judgement is passed the millennium will begin; 5. The second advent of Christ will occur before the millennium; 6. the 1260 years of Daniel 7 and Revelation 13 ought to be measured from the reign of Justinian to the French Revolution; 7. the vials of wrath (Revelation 16) are now being poured out and the second advent is imminent.[8]

The publication of the Albury Declaration gave popular support to this elementary outline of premillennialism. A variety of leaders emerged during the succeeding decades, each with his or her particular emphasis, but the Albury outline served as an accurate summary of the movement.

The most influential of the British premillennialists was a Scotsman, John Nelson Darby. Darby emphasized the teaching that history is divided into dispensations and elevated the concept of Israel as the key factor in Bible prophecy. He visited the United States on six occasions between 1852 and 1876 and found eager audiences everywhere he traveled. Darby's influence upon American theology, especially millennarian thought in the U.S., cannot be over-emphasized. His particular brand of premillennialism became a key theological orientation of the Bible and Prophecy Conferences, which molded fundamentalism during the 1875-1920 period.

By the mid-1880's, premillennialism was a major force in American Christianity. The most popular advocate was William E. Blackstone, whose best-selling volume *Jesus is Coming,* was translated into 48 languages. In 1891, Blackstone conceived and directed the first major lobby effort in the United States advocating the establishment a Jewish state in Palestine. His petition campaign received popular support from major newspapers across the United States. The petition itself urged President Benjamin Harrison to respond to Russian pogroms against Jews and settle them in Palestine. It stated in part:

> Why not give Palestine back to them (the Jews) again? According to God's distribution of nations it is their home and inalienable possession from which they were expelled by force.[9]

Blackstone and a network of supporters enlisted signatures from influential Americans in every major city, including newspaper editors, Senators, Congresspersons, clergy, and academics. Among the signators were Chief Justice of the Supreme Court Melville Fuller, hundreds of Roman Catholic and Protestant clergy, plus such business leaders as John D. Rockefeller, J. P. Morgan and Charles B. Scribner. The effort developed independently of the weak and unpopular Zionist movement. It would be many years before the Jewish Zionists could mount such a campaign in the United States, and once they began to work, they stood on the shoulders of the fundamentalist Christian Zionists who preceded them.

Still the most pivotal role to be played by fundamentalist Christian Zionists was to occur in England. Throughout Queen Victoria's reign (1837-1901) the premillennialist movement gained momentum in the churches and among several important advocates within the ruling elite. Perhaps the most influential of the political premillennialists was the seventh Earl of Shaftesbury, whose writings and political work linked the idea of "Jewish Restoration" to Queen Victoria's political agenda: no Jewish settlement in England and the need for a land bridge to Asia and India. It was Shaftesbury who first coined the phrase: "A nation without a country for a country without a nation." The early Zionists transposed his words to "A land of no people for a people with no land."

Two of England's prominent political figures, Lord Arthur Balfour and David Lloyd-George, came to power in time to formulate the policies for Lord Shaftesbury's dream. The conservative Foreign Minister, Lord Balfour had initially opposed Jewish settlement in the British Isles. While he refused to live beside Jews, he claimed to love them as a people, due to his theological predispostion to Christian Zionism. It was Balfour's commitment to Christian Zionism that led him to support a Jewish state in Palestine long before he met the early Zionist leaders Theodor Herzl and Chaim Weitzmann. In 1919, after the Balfour Declaration opened the door to the Zionists' agenda, Balfour wrote that God's plan must be fulfilled "only from this one land, only through this history, only by this one people."[10]

Prime Minister David Lloyd-George, had a more pronounced orientation toward fundamentalist Christian Zionism. Reflecting back upon his Christian up-bringing, Lloyd-George wrote: "I was brought up in a school where I was taught far more about the history of Jews than the history of my own land." The Prime Minister's encouragement to the Zionist movement and his betrayal of the Arabs concerning independence and the future of Palestine are a matter of record.[11]

The tragic flaw in fundamentalist Christian Zionism continues to be its rejection of the indigenous Palestinian Arabs. This anti-Arab form of anti-Semitism remains the curse and unfinished task of both Gentile and Jewish Zionism, whose twin responses of denial and rejection have wrought havoc on these "other" Semites. Until now, the convergence of these parallel strains of Revisionist Zionist mythology have dominated political, intellectual and religious life in North America.

The Revival of Christian Zionism in the U.S.

The establishment of a Jewish state in Palestine (1948) awakened the otherwise moribund premillenialist Christians. However, the true revival of the movement did not begin until well after the Israeli military occupation of the West Bank and East Jerusalem in 1967. While the 1948 and 1967 events triggered a host of prophetic fantasies ranging from the immediate Second Coming of Jesus to World War III, it was the American bicentennial in 1976 that marked the ascendency of fundamentalist Christian Zionism as a political factor.

At least four developments contributed to the Christian Zionist revival in 1976. First, by the early 1970's, the premillennialist-Charismatic wing of Christianity became the fastest growing element in American Christendom. The election of "born again" President Jimmy Carter, who taught Sunday School in his Southern Baptist Church, sent a signal to several political power-brokers that the 45-50 million evangelicals were now a major political force. Such conservative strategists as Ed McAteer of the Religious Roundtable and Rev. Jerry Falwell, destined to lead the Moral Majority, began to mobilize high-tech resources to politicize their formerly apolitical constituencies. Direct mail specialist Richard Vigerie provided much of the technology. Several of America's wealthiest individuals, such as the Hunt family of Dallas, Texas (of silver market speculator fame) provided the financial backing.

Second, the American Jewish Committee, several pro-Israeli lobbys, and major Zionist leaders saw the fundamentalists as their most important ally. Many Zionists de-emphasized their work with mainline Protestant churchs and turned to the fundamentalists, despite the numerous political and ethical contradictions entailed in such a shift. Rabbi Marc H. Tannenbaum, National Interreligious Affairs Director of the American Jewish Committee, summarized the change in this way:

> The evangelical community is the largest and fastest growing block of pro-Israeli, pro-Jewish sentiment in this country. Since the 1967 War, the Jewish community has felt abandoned by Protestants, by groups clustered around the National Council of Churches, which, because of sympathy with third world causes, gave an impression of support for the PLO. There was a vacuum in public support to Israel that began to be filled by the fundamentalist and evangelical Christians.[11]

Tannebaum's comments are a distortion of the actual policies and positions taken by the National Council of Churches and member bodies which, if anything were still decidedly pro-Israel. Yet positions began to emerge, carefully worded so as to be as balanced as possible, but demonstrating a growing awareness of Palestinian rights.

Nevertheless, Tannenbaum and other Zionist leaders sensed that if they were to receive less than 100% pro-Israel support from the mainstream of Protestantism, they would embrace the fundamentalists. In several cases, Zionist organizations assigned staff to cultivate relations among fundamentalists and the broader evangelical community. The Anti-Defamation League in Chicago employed Rabbi

Yeckiel Eckstein until 1984, whose primary task was to monitor and build linkage with the evangelical movement. The Rabbi landed part-time positions in a Baptist Seminary as well as with fundamentalist Baptist leader W. A. Criswell's First Baptist Church of Dallas, Texas (the largest church in the United States). AIPAC (the Israeli lobby) has added a staff person whose purpose is to forge ties with the fundamentalists.

A third factor was the election of Menachem Begin and his Likud Coalition to power in Israel (1977). This dramatic change in rhetoric, if not in acutal policy, gave legitamacy to religious extremism and the use of Biblical references to justify hardline Zionist strategies. Begin and the fundamentalist Christian Zionists in the United States established an immediate alliance and the two proceeded to manipulate each other whenever it proved expedient. The convergence of Revisionist Zionism with a Western government and massive grassroots support from American Christians was now in place.

The fourth development may have been the primary catalyst to accelerate the rate at which the Begin-fundamentalist Christian connection exerted itself as a political force. When newly inaugurated President Jimmy Carter launched his human rights policy and began to discuss the need for a Palestinian "homeland", Mr. Begin and the Zionist apparatus shifted into overdrive to head off a potential tilt toward a Palestinian state. Discussions with the Soviet Union and others concerning an international peace conference on Palestine added fuel to the fire. The long range political answer was to usurp Palestinian rights through the Camp David Accords. However, a series of activities developed immediately with the fundamental Christians.

An important political initiative by the Christian Zionists came in the form of full-page advertisements in major U.S. newspapers titled, "Evangelical Support for Israel." The text stated in part: "The time has come for evangelical Christians to affirm their belief in biblical prophecy and Israel's divine rights to the land." Taking aim at Jimmy Carter's still premature discussions of a Palestinian homeland and an international peace conference, the advertisement went on to state:

> We affirm as evangelicals our belief in the promised land to the Jewish people ... we would view with grave concern any effort to carve out of the Jewish homeland, another nation or political entity.[12]

The campaign was financed and co-ordinated from Jerusalem through the fundamentalist Institute for Holy Land Studies and had endorsements from leading evangelicals such as Pat Boone, Kenneth Kantzer of *Christianity Today,* and Dallas Seminary President John Walvoord.

This important campaign was simply one of several political initiatives undertaken by Christian Zionists thus reflecting the marriage of Christian premillennialist theology to Begin's Revisionist Zionism. The Likud Government was not about to allow a new U.S. administration to alter the Zionist domination of its Middle East policy, particularly when the newly politicized Christian right shared the Eretz Israel myth on Biblical and political grounds.

The evangelical newspaper campaign was co-ordinated in the United States by a former employee of the American Jewish Committee named Jerry Strober, who told *Newsweek:*

> (The evangelicals) are Carter's constituency and he would better listen to them . . . The real source of strength the Jews have in this country is from the evangelicals.[13]

Strober's comments summarize why the Zionist establishment suddenly adopted the Christian right despite it latent anti-Jewish sentiment, racism, and anti-secular humanism. A case in point was the President of the Southern Baptist Convention, Rev. Bailey Smith, who expressed doubt that God hears the prayers of Jews. Smith was quickly taken to Israel by Rabbi Eckstein and returned with a "corrected" message. However, this tension over the right-wing's political agenda will continue to haunt the Zionist establishment for years to come and its tendency to raise an ugly head of anti-Semitism is always just below the surface. (see Appendix B).

Voices for Armageddon

Several fundamentalist organizations, spokespersons, and even Christian Zionist lobby organizations have emerged since 1976 as Israel's Christian advocates in the United States. Here we will not attempt an exhaustive analysis or survey but merely refer to representative organizations and major personalities.

A. The Televangelists: Several fundamentalist preachers have mastered the medium of television and in at least five cases they have developed $50 million-plus operations. There are now three Christian television networks. One organization, the Christian Broadcasting Network (CBN), has a satellite, a television station in South Lebanon, and a Jerusalem News Bureau. Ironically, they cannot broadcast to Israel but the signal is beamed throughout the Arab World and to their primary means of support, the United States. The message of Christian Zionism, both in its premillennialist theology and political forms (the two are indistinguishable) are consistent themes of most televangelists. Foremost among them are Jerry Falwell and Pat Robertson.

1. *The Moral Majority:* Evangelical author Wes Granberg-Michaelson has noted that: "Jerry Falwell is perhaps the first major American political figure to claim that the United States must support Israel not simply for Israel's sake, but because of its own self-preservation. Falwell has been duly rewarded, receiving from Begin in 1979 "The Jabotinsky Award" and more recently an Israeli jet for his personal and business use.[14]

Falwell's Christian Zionism is rooted in his premillennialist theology and his ultra-conservative politics. As an ardent anti-Communist crusader, Falwell advocates the incomparable value of Israel as the only "democracy" in the region. According to this position, the U.S. must provide the necessary military support to keep the Soviets out (and U.S. "in"). Falwell's political views are buttressed by quotes from the Bible and major premillennialist doctrines which he outlines in his book, *Listen America.* Falwell devotes an entire chapter to Israel which is summarized in a single quotation, "To stand against Israel is to stand against God."[15]

Falwell's message of Christian Zionism is proclaimed through a variety of vehicles including his television program, "The Old Time Gospel Hour," a daily radio program and the political lobby The Moral Majority. The newsletter, *Moral Majority Report* now claims 2.5 million readers including 82,000 clergy, every Senator, Congressperson, Governor, and all major media in the country.

A frequent visitor to Israel, Falwell holds an annual Holy Land tour plus a Bible-Prophecy Conference in Jerusalem. The 1985 version was held in late February to early March and involved five planeloads of tourists. Two participants in the previous tour (November 1983) summarized the experience as a minimum of Christianity with a maximum of Israeli propaganda, including keynote political speeches from the Defense Minister Arens and others. Participants were instructed by their Israeli tour guides, upon departing Nazareth for Jerusalem, via the West Bank, to close their eyes and go to sleep because there was nothing of importance to see.

An oft neglected result of the November 1983 tour was the formation of a Moral Majority sister organization in Israel called "The New Israeli Right." It is modeled after its American parent and is designed to produce Revisionist Zionist policies in Israeli society. Its founder, Avigdor Eskin, is a member of Rabbi Kahane's Kach Movement and was banned from Israeli politics after several arrests for attacks on Palestinian families from his base in the fanatical Kiryat Arba settlement. Eskin turned to Falwell who guaranteed major financial support.[16]

In early April, 1985, Falwell claimed the success of his campaign to turn former critic of Israel, Sen. Jesse Helms, into a new "convert to Israel." Helm's dramatic switch marked yet another political effect of the Christian Zionists campaign and provides further evidence of the movement's value to Israel.

2. *The 700 Club and CBN:* Undoubtedly, the most sophisticated and influential televangelist is Pat Robertson, whose Christian Broadcasting Network began as a tiny Christian television station in Portsmouth, Virginia in 1961. Today Robertson's enterprise claims a massive international TV network complete with a satellite and international correspondents. Programs are beamed into 25 countries through equipment representing the latest in broadcasting technology. Robertson's CBN University is his latest venture in hi-tech Christian communications. His April 10, 1982 purchase of Star of Hope television from evangelist George Otis (who worked closely with the renegade Lebanese Major Saad Haddad) gave CBN new possibilities in the Middle East.

Robertson and his associates at CBN are clearly political and could not be more intentional in their advocacy of Israel. During the Israeli invasion of Lebanon in 1982, Robertson appealed to 700 Club viewers to write President Reagan so that he would free the Israeli army to go as far into Lebanon as they deemed necessary. A Richmond (Virginia) Times-Dispatch report on CBN in 1979 stated: ("Robertson's) advisors unabashedly explain that CBN is a Zionist organization." The reporter also noted that CBN tax returns indicate that the organization contributes heavily to the United Jewish Appeal and Israeli Bonds.[17]

CBN's violations of the Federal Communications Commission regulations, particularly the fairness doctrine, has not yet received a serious test. During 1983, the American Arab Anti-Discrimination Committee challenged CBN's abuse of the airwaves and its pro-Israeli political activity but no legal action has been taken.

B. Christian Zionist Lobbies: The "televangelists" have a series of conservative issues to communicate to their viewers. Although Israel is often at the top of their lists, Christian Zionist lobbies focus upon nothing but Israel.

1. Mike Evans and "Jerusalem DC (David's Capitol):" Israel's current "rising star" among the fundamentalists is a self-proclaimed Middle East expert and evangelist from Texas named Mike Evans. Ironically, Evans is a Christian premillennialist minister in the Assemblies of God denomination and is also Jewish (his mother is an Orthodox Jew). Evans perceives himself as having a divine mission from God which he describes as "I have been called to shake America and Israel for God."[18]

Evans trumpets his intimacy with Israeli political officials and proudly proclaims that he has met with Prime Minister Begin more than any American evangelist. On a recent audio-tape and television special titled, "Israel, America's Key to Survival," Evans notes that he was apprised of the Invasion of Lebanon two days before it occurred, while he was praying with Mr. Begin.[19]

Perhaps more frightening for Americans is a quote from Evans' 1983 fundraising letter:

> Little did I know that the President of the United States would invite me to the White House or that God would stand me up to challenge 58 generals and admirals with the truth of God in the middle of a White House meeting . . . or lit-

tle did I know a speech written by me, calling America to stand by Israel, would be put into the Congressional Record.[20]

Mike Evans' latest venture is a one-hour television special titled, JERUSALEM DC (DAVID'S CAPITOL)." Between October, 1984 and April, 1985 it aired on approximately 250 television stations. Its initial thrust was to reach evangelical voters prior to the Presidential election and the impending vote on moving the U.S. Embassy to Jerusalem. The film was revised and aired again in January, most likely to soften American taxpayers for Israel's gargantuan aid request to the U.S. Congress and gather support for another initiative the Embassy legislation.

*2. The International Christian Embassy in Jerusalem (ICEJ):*On September 30, 1980, the International Christian Embassy opened its doors in a fashionable section of West Jerusalem to declare: "Jerusalem is the undivided, eternal, capital of Israel." The opening occurred shortly after Israel illegally annexed East Jerusalem, and thirteen nations responded by closing their Jerusalem embassies. Nevertheless, Jerusalem Mayor Teddy Kollek and other dignitaries turned out to give their blessings to this unique fundamentalist Christian Zionist operation.

Supported by the Israeli government and fundamentalist churches from South Africa, Europe, and the United States, the Embassy conducts such programs as: an international prayer and information network to support Israeli politics; petition drives and marches; press conferences; direct-mail campaigns; organizing a September celebration which draws 5000 Christians to Jerusalem; the promotion of Israeli-made products and selling Israeli bonds to American churches; Holy Land tours; and blood donations to the IDF (during the 1982 invasion of Lebanon). There are now Christian Embassies in 37 countries throughout Europe, North America, Asia, and Australia. Plans include several additional offices, particularly across the United States, where there are an estimated 20 embassies. In August, 1985, the Christian Embassy will organize a Christian Zionist convention in Basle, Switzerland, which was the site of the first world Zionist convention of 1897.

Despite its unquestionably Revisionist Zionist orientation and public support from such Israeli leaders as Begin, Arens, Shamir, Kollek, and others, the ICEJ has come under intense fire from fanatical Rabbis Kahane, and Levinger. Many Israelis are aware of the fundamentalist's propensity for proselytizing, such as the city planner who told the *Chicago Tribune:* "Nothing could be more humiliating than that the Jewish state, which was forged on the fires of anti-Semitism, would allow Christians to evangelize here."[21]

As the militant Zionists and their followers continue to rise in Israeli politics and gain popular support, life may become increasingly difficult for Christian Zionist within Israel. Of greater concern is the enmity stirred up by the ICEJ that triggers Zionists attacks on Arab Christian and Muslim clergy and institutions. The reports of arson, bombings, rape, and even murder by Jewish terrorists have escalated since 1980. In addition, there is a marked increase in Christian-Muslim tensions among Palestinians, a dynamic relatively unknown to Palestinians throughout their history. Thus the ICEJ and similar groups can play into Israel's hands by stirring religious hatred within Palestinian communities, and thus serve as another means of weakening important elements of Palestinian unity and communal life.

C. Christian Zealots and the Temple Mount: On March 10, 1983, a group of 45 Zionist extremists were arrested in Jerusalem on charges that they attempted to seize control, if not blow up the Dome of the Rock. Three weeks later a quarter page advertisement appeared in the *Jerusalem Post* calling for the release of the 45 and praising them as "earnest, faithful sons of Israel" whose arrest is "Biblically unconscionable." The advertisement was placed by an unknown organization calling itself "The Committee of Concerned Evangelicals for Freedom of Worship on the Temple Mount."

The three co-chairmen of the committee are fundamentalist Christian Zionists: Terry Risenhoover, an Oklahoma oil magnate; California businessman Chuck Krieger; and Houston clergyman Rev. James DeLoach. The "Evangelical Committee" is the American counterpart to the militant Jewish Temple Foundation, whose stated goal is the destruction of the Dome of the Rock and rebuilding the Third Temple in its place. In most interpretations of premillennialist theology, the rebuilding of the Temple is one of the last signs prior to Jesus' Second Coming and Armageddon. Risenhoover and Krieger have business ventures in Israel and South Africa, and have been drilling for oil on the West Bank. Possessing extensive financial resources and needing tax shelters, they recently established the Institute for Research for the Temple of Jerusalem, which is registered in the United States as a 510-08-64 tax-exempt organization according to the Internal Revenue Service.

In 1983 Risenhoover and Krieger transferred a minimum of $50,000 to Stanley Goldfoot.[22] Goldfoot, a South African Jew, was one of the most ruthless Stern Gang terrorists of the 1940's and is now linked to the Gush Emunim and Kach movements. Supporting their efforts in the Knesset is the Israeli Minister of Science and Development, Yuval Neeman, who placed a resolution before the Cabinet on March 13, 1983 to allow Jews to pray anywhere in the Temple Mount.

An associate of the Risenhoover-Krieger group, Rev. Chuck Smith, a Baptist pastor from Costa Mesa, California, stated during an interview:

> Do you want a real radical? Try Stanley Goldfoot. He's a wonder. His plan for the Temple Mount is to take sticks of dynamite and some M-16s, and blow up the Dome of the Rock and Al-Aqsa Mosque, and just lay claim to the site.[23]

Rev. Smith's enthusiasm for Goldfoot was outdone only by his hosting the Temple Mount fanatic in his church for a fundraising event, encouraging his 3000 parishioners to pledge financial support for the man who would like to bring on Armageddon. We would also note that a May 1983 poll by the Israeli newspaper *Ha'aretz* indicated that 18.3% of Israelis polled wanted to see construction on the Third Temple begin immediately.

The Risenhoover-Krieger team appear to have direct access to the White House and State Department, and like Mike Evans, are pressing their Armageddon scenario with the Reagan administration. A recent example of their access was a March 19, 1984 White House briefing and reception with over 150 Christian fundamentalist leaders and heads of major American Zionist organizations. Zionist leaders included AIPAC founder I.L. Kennan; the Executive Director for Americans for a Safe Israel; the President of the World Zionist Organization; and over 50 others. The Christian Zionist leadership list read like a "Who's Who" of the movement, with author Hal Lindsay, televangelists Jimmy Swaggert and Jim Bakker, political strategists Tim LaHaye and Ed McAteer, and several others. Not a single Black, Hispanic, Roman Catholic, Orthodox, Arab, or mainline Protestant Christian was invited. The briefing was led by four top Reagan spokesmen in the State Department with J. William Middendorf, U.S. Representative to the Organization of American States, speaking on administration policy in Central America. Bud McFarlane, a high-ranking State Department official and Chief Middle East negotiator spoke on the Middle East. Chairman for the event was the President of American Forum for Jewish-Christian Co-operation, who is none other than Terry Risenhoover. Invitations were sent on State Department stationery and signed by Middendorf. The costly event was a major effort by the Reagan Administration and the Christian and Jewish Zionist organizations to signal their constituencies that this President supported their agendas.

* * * * * *

The above survey merely touches upon some of the historic and contemporary highlights that constitute the powerful fundamentalist Christian Zionist leadership and its political impact. It is readily apparent that Gentile Zionists, particularly those Christians of the premillennialist orientation, have in the past and will continue to provide an important base of political, economic, and ideological support for the state of Israel. The organizations and networks openly collaborate with the Israeli government serving as advocates for a foreign government within the churches through direct mail campaigns, and on their television and radio programs. No one has scientifically measured their impact in direct relation to Israel's political support in the United States but the Zionist leadership themselves admit that they form the single most important bloc of support for Israel (in the U.S.). As Israel faces increased economic and political turmoil, one can only expect increased campaigns and political organizing to secure this critical base of support. In conclusion, I would remind the reader that the fundamentalist Christian Zionists represent only the most visible element of the 50-60 million evangelical Christians in the United States. At best, they may account for one-third of this total, in actual fact, it could be much lower. There is an increasing opposition to their forcing a generally unacceptable conservative political agenda on America, and the push to "Christianize" American government runs counter to the separation of church and state principle upheld by most evangelicals. Nevertheless, the Christian Zionists underscore the fact that American powerbrokers have generally accepted Zionist myths concerning the Holy Land and have inherited a curse of anti-Arab, anti-Semitism toward the Palestinians. The failure of American Christians and the intellectual community to demythologize the distortions of Revisionist Zionism remain an overwhelming burden for the forseeable future.

Footnotes

1. Timothy Weber, *Living in the Shadow of the Second Coming*, Grand Rapids, Zondervan Publishing House, 1983, pg. 13. See also Peter Grose, *Israel in the Mind of America*, New York: Alfred A. Knopl, 1983, p. 37.

2. Hal Lindsay, *The Promise*, Eugene Oregon, Harvest Publications, 1982, pg. 199.

3. Barbara Tuchman *Bible and Sword*, New York: Simon and Schuster, 1983

4. Regina Sharif, *Non-Jewish Zionism*, (London, Zed Press, 1983).

5. LeRoy Froom, *The Prophetic Faith of Our Fathers*, Washington Review and Herald Press, 1954, p. 137.

6. Ernest Sandeen, *The Roots of Fundamentalism*, Chicago: The University of Chicago Press, 1970, p. 19.

8. *Ibid.*, p. 42.

9. For a more detailed account see Sandeen, *Ibid*, p. 19.

10. Lord Arthur Balfour, "Introduction" to Sokolow's *History of Zionism*, London, 1919.

11. David Lloyd-George, in a speech to the Jewish Historical Society of England, 25 May, 1925, recorded in Christopher Sykes, *Two Studies in Virtue*. New York: Alfred A. Knopf, 1952, p. 193.

12. Washington Post, 23 March, 1981.

13. Advertisment, *The Christian Science Monitor*, 3 November 1977.

14. William Claibourne, "Israelis Look on U.S. Evangelical Christians as Potent Ally," *Washington Post*, 23 March 1981.

15. Grace Halsell, in a speech at the conference "The Palestine Question and the American Churches," Chicago, 20 January 1984.

15. Jerry Falwell, *Listen America*, New York: Doubleday and Company, 1980, p. 215.

16. Yehudit Vinkler, "The New Israeli Right." *Ha-aretz*, 3 November, 1983.

17. Ed Briggs, "Nation Put at Pinnacle of God's Plan, (*Richmond Times-Dispatch*) 2 May 1979.

18. Mike Evans Ministries Fundraising Letter, Fall 1983, Bedford, Texas.

19. Mike Evans audio cassette, "Israel, America's Key to Survival," Bedford, Texas, 1984.
20. Fundraising Letter, *Ibid.*
21. *Chicago Tribune,* March 21, 1983.
22. Sol Stern, "the Neo-Conning of the Jews," *Village Voice,* 4 September 1984.
23. Grace Halsell, "The Temple Mount Plot," *The Link,* New York: Americans for Middle East Understanding, 1984.

Ronald Reagan's 'Theology' of Armaggedon

BY LARRY JONES AND GERALD T. SHEPPARD

"Pie-in-the-sky" religion is condemned by progressive evangelicals for its lack of political concern, a willingness to postpone issues of social justice in order to meditate on events during the period of the Great Tribulation. So-called "apocalyptic" eschatology appears to be pre-occupied with "things to come," and pays little attention to the way things actually are. Such a neat distinction between piety and politics often proves to be an illusion. Even apocalyptic ideas have direct political consequences for those who hold to them and to the *politeia* who are under their authority or influence. So, too, American politicians have often recognized a connection between public policy and their religious views. More than any other American president in recent history, Ronald Reagan has displayed a keen interest in biblical prophecy. His interest is evidently more than academic, for he has linked a number of political decisions to biblical prophetic scenario familiar to fundamentalist dispensationalism.

Charismatic Christians close to Reagan, Christian journalists, long-time friends and Reagan himself have made reference to the president's interest in prophecy. Reagan met with friends for an afternoon of fellowship on September 20, 1970 to talk about the Holy Spirit and the signs of the unfolding apocalyptic drama. The meeting is described in George Otis's 1971 book *High Adventure* and in Bob Slosser's 1984 *Reagan Inside/Out.*

After his appearance at a charismatic clinic in Sacramento, Pat Boone, his wife Shirley and two friends, George Otis and Harold Bredesen, drove to the Reagan home. Pat Boone told the Reagans of his recent experiences with the Holy Spirit, including the new song he had sung "in tongues." Recent headlines told of civil war in Jordan and Nixon threatened intervention. Reagan listened intently to his old friend.

At some point, Reagan turned the conversation to the subject of Bible prophecy. He told his guests of a story he had heard from Billy Graham. The famous evangelist, a longtime friend of Reagan, told him of a talk he had with Conrad Adenauer. The then West German chancellor had asked Graham what the next great news event would be. Graham shrewdly answered, "The return of Jesus Christ."

Reagan, then, listed what he saw as the signs of the times: The scattering of the Jews, the re-gathering of Israel in 1948, and, most especially, the Israeli capture of Jerusalem in 1967. Reagan saw the stage being set for the last act in world history. George Otis described Reagan's using the Bible as a signpost or chronometer of history. For Reagan, the Old Testament prophecies marked the rise and the fall of empires in the timeline of world history. The Bible seemed to him to have authenticated itself by virtue of the complex and intricate "*fulfillment of many prophecies*." Otis reported that Reagan delighted in the wonderful cadence of history marching with such beauty and precision. Bredesen told the governor that he had failed to mention the most important sign of all, namely, the

Reprinted with permission from *TSF Bullentin*, Sept.-Oct. 1984, pp. 16-19. Larry Jones is a graduate student at Columbia University and Gerald Sheppard is associate professor of Old Testament at Union Theological Seminary, New York.

two great Pentecosts, one of Satan and one of God, which mark the present time as the "last days."

The trial of the cultic Manson murders had only recently filled the television screens and newspaper headlines. For their last fifteen minutes together the little group spoke fervently of their experiences with the Holy Spirit. Pat Boone gave his old Hollywood friend an enscribed copy of his recent book *A New Song*. Boone, Otis, and Bredesen presented Reagan with a copy of an apocalyptic pamphlet they had written, *A Solution to Crisis America.* Before they left the Reagan home, someone suggested they pray together. They joined hands in a circle. In the course of his prayer, George Otis was "possessed by the Holy Spirit." Otis or the Spirit possessing Otis addressed Reagan as "my son" and prophesied that Reagan would one day be "resident of 1600 Pennsylvania Avenue." Otis' left hand, the one holding Reagan's right, began to shake and pulsate. Everyone opened their eyes and let go of one another's hands. Ellingwood drove away in the waiting limousine with the visitors. He told them on the ride back to Sacramento that while he held Reagan's left hand, it, also, shook and pulsated when Otis prayed. Later he reported having felt a "bolt of electricity" from Reagan's hand.[1]

Possibly the first published evidence of Reagan's interest in biblical prophecy appeared in the May, 1968 *Christian Life.* In the lead article Reagan's pastor, Donn Moomaw, told of a visit he and Billy Graham had had with Ronald Reagan while he was in the hospital. They became engrossed in a discussion of "Bible prophecy in relation to the signs of the times." The writer, William Rose, confirmed that meeting with Governor Reagan. Reagan said,

> We got into a conversation about how many of the prophecies concerning the Second Coming seemed to be having their fulfillment at this time. Graham told me how world leaders who are students of the Bible and others who have studied it have come to his same conclusion—that apparently never in history have so many of the prophecies come true in such a relatively short time.

Reagan added that he had asked Moomaw for more material on prophecy in order to check it out in the Bible for himself. Reagan's keen interest in biblical prophecy seems to have been especially incited by the 1967 re-unification of Jerusalem.

In October, 1983, President Reagan made an apocalyptic telephone remark to Tom Dine, executive director of the American-Israeli public affairs committee. The remark was published, first, by the Jerusalem Post and then picked up by the Associated Press. Reagan told the pro-Israel lobbyist,

> You know, I turn back to your ancient prophets in the Old Testament and the signs for telling Armaggedon, and I find myself wondering if—if we're the generation that is going to see that come about. I don't know if you've noted any of those prophecies lately, but believe me they certainly describe the times we're going through.

Reagan telephoned Dine to thank him for lobbying efforts of AIPAC to secure votes in favor of continued U.S. military presence in Lebanon. The U.S. embassy in Beirut had only recently been destroyed by a terrorist bomb. Only days after President Reagan's aside to Dine, a similar terrorist attack killed 279 U.S. marines near the Beirut airport.

Later, reporters from *People Magazine*, Dec. 6, 1983, asked Reagan about his remark. According to the transcript published in the weekly compilation of presidential documents, Reagan then asked them where it had been published:

> The President: Where was that?
>
> Question: In the Jerusalem Post. And I was going to say, Is this really true? Do you believe that?
>
> The President: I've never done that publicly. I have talked here, and then

> I wrote people because some theologians, quite some time ago were telling me, calling attention to the fact that theologians had been studying the ancient prophecies—What would portend the coming the Armageddon?—and have said that never, in the time between the prophecies up until now has there ever been a time in which so many of the prophecies are coming together. There have been times in the past when people thought the end of the world was coming, and so forth, but never anything like this. And one of them, the first one who ever broached this to me—and I won't use his name; I don't have permission to. He probably would give it, but I'm not going to ask—had held a meeting with the then head of the German government years ago when the war was over, and did not know that his hobby was theology. And he asked this theologian what did he think was the next great news event worldwide. And the theologian, very wisely, said, "Well, I think that you're asking that question in because you've had a thought along the line." And he did. It was about the prophecies and so forth. So no. I've talked conversationally about that.
>
> Question: You've mused on it. You've considered it.
>
> The President: (laughing) Not to the extent of throwing up my hands and saying, "Well, it's all over." No. I think whichever generation and at whatever time, when the time comes, the generation that is there, I think will have to go on doing what they believe is right.
>
> Question: Even if it comes?
>
> The President: Yes.

Two years earlier, while President Reagan was lobbying Congress for AWAC surveillance aircraft for Saudi Arabia, he talked with Senator Howell Hefflin of Alabama about biblical prophecy. Senator Hefflin told reporters:

> We got off into the Bible a little bit. We were talking about the fact that the Middle East, according to the Bible, would be the place where Armaggedon would start. The President was talking to me about the Scriptures and I was talking a little to him about the Scriptures. He interprets the Bible and Armaggedon to mean that Russia is going to get involved in it.[2]

On another occasion, according to the *New York Times, President Reagan euphemistically named the MX missile, a first strike weapon, "the peacemaker." His aides objected that this biblically based euphemism was too easily confused with "pacemaker," a word with an unpleasant connotation. Reagan obliqued and changed the missile's name to "peacekeeper," a word which more properly invokes images of old west shoot-outs rather than the Sermon on the Mount.*

Herbert Ellingwood, chairman of the Federal Merit System Protection, and longtime Reagan aide, recently told a reporter that Reagan has read and repeatedly discussed Hal Lindsey's *Late Great Planet Earth*. Reagan apparently believes in the apocalyptic scenario popularized by Lindsey, Falwell, and a host of other fundamentalist dispensationalists. According to this scenario,the Gog-Magog war will be a Soviet invasion of Israel. The invading Soviets and their allies will be crushed either by God or the U.S. nuclear arsenal, used as a tool in the hand of God. That war sets the stage for an Anti-christ, totalitarian regime. At the end of seven years of Tribulation, Jesus will come again to defeat the Anti-christ and to establish his millennial kingdom.

George Otis, who prophesied Reagan's presidency in 1970, believes that an Arab-Israeli war will trigger the "Gog-Magog" conflagration in which God/America will destroy the Soviet military machine. Otis writes in his 1974 book, *The Ghost of Hagar*:

> The Bible clearly says that this movement WILL still take place one day in

> the near future. When will this be? Could it be during 'War Number Five' coming up against Israel? The early percolating of War Number Five has already begun. (Otis emphasis).

Otis foresees America coming to the rescue of Israel. "America," he writes, "will be blessed for her sacrificial role during Israel's crisis hour."

Translated into real political terms, this scenario means, arguably, a preemptive American first strike against a perceived Soviet attack on Israel. In order to protect Israel, the U.S. must defeat Russia. In order to "win" the war, a nuclear first strike is necessary. America's "sacrifice" would be the destruction caused by the Soviet second strike retaliation. But Otis hopes to be raptured out before the bombs explode.

George Otis is a former electronics manufacturer who made nuclear weapon system components. He now devotes his time to his "High Adventure" ministry and operated four radio stations in southern Lebanon. The late Major Hadad, a Phalangist leader, was a close associate of Otis. Otis' "Voice of Hope" radio devotes part of its programming to the Phalangist line. He first met Reagan the day he uttered his presidential prophecy. He interviewed Reagan in the 1976 presidential campaign and again during the 1980 presidential campaign Otis was honorary chairman of "Christians for Reagan," an offshoot of Christian Voice.

On a number of occasions during the 1980 campaign, candidate Regan remarked that "this may be the last generation." Dispensationalists like Hal Lindsey and Tim LaHaye are board members of Christian Voice, which has rallied support for Reagan's moral agenda. For the 1984 presidential campaign, LaHayes's "American Coalition for Traditional Values" (ACTV) is organizing a highly selective, voter registration drive to bring out the "born again" vote. Otis said in a recent interview that Reagan's re-election, "could make a difference in the timing of Jesus' return."

In 1981 Reagan's appointee, James Watt, then Secretary of the Interior, told a House Committee, "I don't know how many future generations we can count on before the Lord returns." Watts remark raised a furor and resulted in perhaps some unfair parody. Watt made his statement so casually because fundamentalist dispensationalists view the coming Tribulation as a time of purifying violence will cleanse the earth for her millennial replenishment. George Otis, in his 1974 *Millennial Man*, writes, "Earth needs and will soon get her Millennium overhaul." For Otis, as apparently for Watt, the energy crisis was also a sign of divine providence:

> Before all the earth's gears lock up for want of lubrication, this age will close. The oil supplies which God placed in the planet will prove adequate to squeak through this era.

The earth, Otis writes,

> needs to be born again. but before it can, there must be a clearing away of everything decadent. Our all-wise Heavenly Father knows He must 'PLOW UP THE EARTH,' root out and eliminate everything that won't harmonize with His Millennial-life blueprint.

As Otis sees it, the earth must be destroyed first and then Jesus will return with his saints to "re-plant, re-build, and re-organize." This is the same Otis who, in his 1976 T.V. interview with candidate Reagan, asked

> Governor Reagan, concerning another country that is extremely unique . . . Perhaps the most dramatic Bible prophecy which has been fulfilled right in our own day is the re-emergence of Israel as a nation. What do you feel America should do if ever in the future, Israel were about to be destroyed by attacking enemy nations?

Reagan answered,

> Well, here again we have a relationship. We have a pledge to Israel to the preservation of that nation. They are an ally and have been a longtime friend and ally and, again, I think we keep our commitments. I think there is a tendency today that goes along with the things you were mentioning earlier in our talk about the easy way and there are many people taking advantage of the war weariness that came from Vietnam, that long conflict. There are many people who would like to say that, that no agreement is worth keeping if it causes trouble to ourselves. We can't live this way; we have an obligation, a responsibility , and a destiny. We are the leader of the free world and I think, to a certain extent, in the last few years we have tended to abdicate that leadership. A very definite withdrawal from moral commitments.

President Reagan has frequently spoken of "God's plan" for America but has not publicly elaborated what he believes God's plan to be. Reagan delighted many evangelicals with his call for a national revival and his own public testimony to Jesus Christ. Privately, the president has talked repeatedly of his belief in an imminent "Gog-Magog war" involving the Soviet Union. Does the president believe that God has planned a national revival before the Tribulation and then an American sacrificial role in a nuclear God-Magog war? Just what the president's thinking is on the question of the secret Rapture is unknown. The president has, in a 1984 public speech to the National Religious Broadcasters, quoted from post-tribulationist Pat Robertson's *Secret Kingdom*. The apocalyptic coalition supporting Reagan includes the entire pre-, mid-, post-tribulationist spectrum. Reagan's longtime friends Pat Boone and Billy Graham are pre-tribulationists. But the difference betwen pre- and mid-tribulational views is sometimes left up in the air. The people in Reagan's eschatological support group have learned to agree to disagree on certain nuances. Regardless, presidential beliefs in matters of biblical prophecy become a public issues if he sanctions, even by his public silence, this eschatological rationalization for the nuclear build-up for what seems to his supporters to be an inevitable nuclear conflict in the Near East.

Certainly Reagan's fundamentalist dispensational views, obtained through popular literature, like that of Hal Lindsey and George Otis, shold not be equated with the essence of "apocalyptic" interpretation. While not rejecting the value of apocalyptic literature in the Bible, an evangelical New Testament scholar, George Ladd, wrote one of the more persuasive criticisms of these particular dispensational claims in his *The Blessed Hope*. Some Marxists associate themselves with apocalyptic expectation, and a major contemporary theologian, Jurgen Moltmann, has persistently placed a positive stress on apocalyptic themes in his "theology of hope." Black theologian James Cone has similarly spelled out the importance of the "eschatological and future expectation" essential to the black church's understanding of the salvation story, often in terms of "the gospel train."[3] Moreover, " dispensational" views can be found from the time of Augustine and in the work of John Calvin as a way to express views of God's progressive revelation in different periods of history. However, Reagan's statements reflect a particular type of dispensationalism which has only been an option in Christianity since a little more than a century ago.

For example, prior to the nineteenth-century, no figure in church history advocated the belief in a "pre-tribulation rapture."[4] This doctrine finds its origin in the prophetic studies of J. N. Darby in the 1830's. Yet, now in the twentieth-century, the publishing success of *The Late Great Planet Earth* has given the impression to the public that this position is one commonly accepted by biblical and theological scholars in seminaries across the country. The opposite is the case. In fact, most scholars have for so long ignored the whole position that many would not know the intricacy of its terms enough to refute it. They may be correctly challenged to take more seriously the popular views within the church and to address more adequately the eschatological questions too often casually side-stepped in seminary lectures and sermons, but they know that these views have almost no standing among their seminary colleagues.

In Timothy Weber's recent study of dispensationalism, he observes that the popularity of prophecy conferences during the last half of the nineteenth-century had subsided by the beinning of the twentieth-century because premillennarian views lacked any consensus among evangelicals. Nevertheless, World War I attracted renewed attention to matters of biblical prophecy and the dispensational pre-millennialist claimed that the break-up of the Ottoman empire confirmed exactly their predictions based on Scripture. By 1919 prophecy conferences gained renewed popularity and sprouted up across the country. Favorite teachers and their elaborate, colored charts sought to diagnose the future of world politics.[5] Eschatological charts carried their own psychological apologetic, often more persuasive than the technical arguments, for instance, between C. I. Scofield and H. A. Ironside, over the exact nature of "literal interpretation" and how strictly one must distinguish between the church and Israel in Scripture for "the system" to be exegetically sound. Many pentecostal groups, for example, adopted dispensational outlooks corresponding to these charts but generally neither understood nor endorsed the underlying hermeneutic of Scripture which justified the charts.[6]

Because of the timing and success of these new prophecy conferences after the World War I, Weber notes,

> By 1920 premillennialist revivalists could afford to repress their doctrine, while before then they had been careful to remember premillennarialism's distinct minority status within the evangelical mainstream.[7]

If one can, as historian E. Sandeen has argued, think of "fundamentalism" as a movement in reaction to "higher criticism" from the 1860's, it was only in the 1920's that the term "fundamentalist" was invented to describe a wedding of conservative historical views of Scripture on one hand, with a pretribulation rapture, premillennarian estimate of biblical prophecy on the other.

Weber, and Lewis Wilson is his *Armaggedon Now*, review the ensuing history of speculation by fundamentalist dispensationalists regarding current events through the outbreak of World War II, the founding of the state of Israel, the cold war with Russia, and the present period of increasing nuclear tensions.[8] Of course, everyone has a right, perhaps an obligation, to try to estimate what will happen in the future. The very symbolism of the endtimes within biblical prophecy invites a yearning for more precise revelation about the future of this planet. At this point, in our judgment, fundamentalists exhibit their most serious misuse of Scripture. By insisting on a rigorous, historical type of literalistic exegesis of the Bible, they strive to secure additional information hidden from the ordinary reader in the ambiguity of apocalyptic texts. They think they can peep behind veils which were not drawn aside for the author of the book of revelation. But this dispensationalist approach, again, in our judgment, misconstrues the nature of "sensus literalis" of Scripture, for literal interpretation of a "symbol" must *sustain* the text as symbolic or it ceases from being, any longer, "literal." Unless a biblical text is really a secret code (perhaps of parables, cf.Lk. 8:10) which only the insiders rightly understand, then the very power of symbolic text lies in their multi-valency, their endless ability to contribute to the imagery and imagination of faith without allowing a single translation to end their symbolic interpretation once and for all or in favor of *our own* views of the world.

Only the return of Jesus Christ could end the symbolic interpretation of these apocalyptic prophecies in the same way as did the person and work of Christ in the first-century regarding the Christian eschatological interpretations of the Hebrew Bible. A prime example of the danger in premature speculation, like that proffered by so many fundamentalist dispensationalists, can perhaps be found in the Gospel story of Peter's confession of Jesus in Matt. 16:13-23. Recall how Jesus posed the key question to his disciples, "Who do men say that the Son of man is?'' After other disciples volunteer various opinions, Peter responds with the confession, ''You are the Christ (lit. ''the messiah''), the Son of the Living God: (v. 16). Jesus seems elated: ''Blessed are you, Simon Bar Jona!'' We next find the classic text in which Peter is given the so-called ''power of the keys'' and made the rock upon which a future Christian church will be built.

Then, in this new atmosphere of understanding, Jesus begins to tell his disciples for the first time that he wil suffer, die and be resurrected. Immediately, the same Peter, in some sense relying upon his own orthodox eschatology chart regarding the future of the Messiah, rebuffs Jesus, ''God forbid, Lord! This shall never happen to you.'' (v. 22b). This disciple whom Jesus had just blessed, then received the strongest rebuke ever given a disciple:''Get behind me, Satan! You are a hindrance to me; for you are not on the side of God, but of men.'' (v. 23). While Peter may have had the correct christology, he had a wrongly presumptuous eschatology which reduced the mystery of God's revelation to his own literalistic assessment of biblical prophecy. Modern views to the degree that they venture the same presumption, often at the price of marginalizing even the ''plain'' teaching of Jesus, invite the same rebuke from God who will surprise us and in whose hands the future must remain. The idea that America as a nation could tempt Jesus to return by offering him the burnt sacrifice of a world-in-nuclear-flames is a blasphemous parody of Christianity. Prophecy was never offered to sanction such an attack on creation.

The symbolism of prophecy checks those who cannot withstand surprises or mysteries deeper than any flicker of light within a crystal ball. If Augustine can describe even a creed as ''a fence around a mystery,'' a symbolic fence around a mystry like that found in the apocalyptic writings of the Bible ought to make us more cautious than ever.

Our concern with Reagan's comments are, finally, twofold. First, the popular literature upon which he relies on is for us theologically dangerous and presumptuous, risking a rebuke from God like Christ gives to Peter. Of course, this theological critique does not depreciate either the value of apocalyptic literature in Scripture or the necessity of hope, with freedom to imagine what the future might portend. Second, an equally serious concern is that Reagan has been linking these speculative, fundamentalist views of Bible prophecy to his pragmatic vision of the world and to the role his presidential policies play in it. It is one thing to speculate about implications of Bible prophecy, it is another to take one's speculation as seriously as established facts which then can be cited in support of one's politicial decisions. Reagan has been cautious not to voice his position on biblical prophecy in major public speeches, but he has, at a minimum, confirmed a connection between prophecy and some of his policies to insiders in a casual but direct manner. Moreover, Reagan has openly supported the fundamentalist dispensationalist teachers, like George Otis and Jerry Falwell, who then publicize their special rapport with the President on these matters and leave no doubt that a ballot cast for Reagan is a vote for the right team in the final World Series of these last days.

In sum, not every fundamentalist dispensationalist crosses the line from speculation to confident prediction regarding contemporary political events. But the history of dispensationalists doing so is a long and disturbing one. At stake also is the most difficult issue of how religious belief ought to influence one's decisions in public political office. In 1980, a public confession of being ''born again'' was almost required of serious presidential contenders. We hope that the presidential election in 1984 does not become a mandate to experimentally test the dispensationalist hypothesis with a war of our own making.

NOTES

1.The description of Reagan's meeting with Boone, Otis, Bredesen, and Ellingwood is a composite drawn from published statements and especially through interviews by Joe Cuomo of WBAI, New York City. Cuomo and, at times, Larry Jones, have had extensive telephone conversations about these matters with Otis, Bredesen, and Ellingwood. References to "a reporter" primarily have Cuomo in mind. A documentary on the subject, with Larry Jones and Gerald T. Sheppard serving as consultants and commentators, has been aired several times in the New York City area and will, in a revised form, be aired internationally in the next few months. Among the many recently published journalistic investigations on Reagan and eschatology is "Does Reagan Expect a Nuclear Armageddon?" which was the lead editorial in the *Washington Post*, Sunday, April 18, 1984. It was written by Ronnie Dugger, publisher of the *Texas Observor*, with Larry Jones. Another article on the same subject by Dugger and Jones will appear in the next issue of *Mother Jones*.

2.*The New York Times*, Oct. 29, 1981.

3.*God of the Oppressed*, (New York: Seabury Press, 1975), p. 56-57.

4.Timothy Weber, *Living in the Shadow of the Second Coming: American Premillennialism 1875-1925*, (New York: Oxford, 1979), p. 13-42.

5.Smith, p. 21-24.

6.Gerald T. Sheppard, "Pentecostalism and the Hermeneutics of Dispensationalism: The Anatomy of an Uneasy Relationship," p. 1-26, in *Pastoral Problems in the Pentecostal-Charismatic Movement*, ed. by Harold D. Hunter (Cleveland: Church of God School of Theology, 1982). A paper delivered to the Society of Pentecostal Studies, held Nov. 3-5, 1983.

7.Weber, p. 52.

8.Cf., also, E. R. Chamberlin, *Antichrist and the Millennium*, (New York: Saturday Review Press, 1975).

"The Prophet Who Would Be King"

BY DONALD E. WAGNER

In 1983, American Christian televangelist Pat Robertson stated, "We have enough voters to run the country, and when people say, 'We've had enough,'' we are going to take over."[1]

Robertson is now putting the political and economic pieces of that prophecy together as a candidate for the Republican nomination for President of the United States. He is a man driven by a prophetic vision for a Christian America, according to his political and theological views. As the most visible and listened to religious leader in North America, former skeptics are now beginning to believe Robertson may deliver on his 1983 promise—if not in 1988, then perhaps by 1992.

Who is Pat Robertson and where did he come from? Obviously, he did not appear suddenly on the American scene with his current bid for the Republican nomination. Pat Robertson's influence, like his television fortunes, have risen gradually rather than instantaneously over nearly three decades. In order to understand the man and his followers, one needs to review the history and context of this development.

In most ways, Pat Robertson's credentials as an All-American leader are more impressive than those of any president since the Second World War, including Dwight Eisenhower and Ronald Reagan. Robertson is a descendent of the signers of the Declaration of Independence. He is a direct descendent of William Henry and Benjamin Harrison, the ninth and twenty-third Presidents. His father A. Willis Robertson was a U.S. Senator from Virginia and member of Congress for over twenty years.

Pat is a former U.S. Marine and Golden Gloves boxer, as well as a graduate of Yale University Law School. After completing his law studies in 1955 Robertson failed his New York bar exam but entered the business world in New York City. A profound conversion experience during this period led him to enter New York Theological Seminary. Following graduation Pat received a personal call from God that took him to Portsmouth, Virginia, where he purchased a dying UHF television station for the sum of $37,000. When all the papers were signed and Robertson's loan complete, he had $70.00 in his pocket and $36,430 indebetedness. But station WYAH (W-Yahweh, or Hebrew for God) was on the air as the first fully Christian television channel in the United States.

This was the first of many successes, as Robertson's autobiography *Shout It From The Housetops* explains in detail. Television station WYAH is now a network, the Christian Broadcasting Network (CBN) with annual revenues of well over $200 million in 1985.[2] It employs over 4000 people and is the fourth largest network in America. CBN cable is the second largest cable network in the country. In addition, CBN broadcasts to over 60 countries around the world, including a television station in southern Lebanon and news bureau in Jerusalem. CBN Graduate School in Christian Communications enrolls over

725 students and a new law school (acquired from Oral Roberts) opened in September, 1986. A major Christian relief organization, Operation Blessing, funnels over $30 million dollars to conservative political outlets in Africa, Central America and the Middle East, reflecting the foreign policy views of Robertson.

According to an October, 1985 A.C. Nielson Survey, Pat Robertson is now the most visible American religious leader. Over 21 per cent of American households turn their television sets to CBN programs at least 6 minutes each week, and over 40 per cent for a minimum of six minutes each month. Thus, 61 million Americans have at least some minimal exposure to Pat Robertson and his fundamentalist religious and political agenda. This rating places him only slightly behind most prime-time programs on the major television networks.

University of Virginia sociologist Jeffrey K. Hadden minimized the popularity of Robertson and other televangelists in his 1981 study *Prime Time Preachers*. After the 1985 Neilson poll, Hadden commented: "the televangelists have greater unrestricted access to media then any other interest group in America."[3] Hadden and the many analysts who dismissed Robertson have radically altered their initial conclusions and see Robertson as a major force in American religion and politics.

Many analysts are examining the sociological and cultural dimensions of Christian fundamentalism.[4] A distinct fundamentalist Christian subculture has emerged with its own set of political values, private code of morality, political agenda, heroes and enemies. For the devoted flock who follow their leaders, whether the televangelists or local pastors, a distinct life-style and world-view can be discerned.

Pat Robertson and his daily "700 Club" program is a staple for this sub-culture. A 90 minute television talk show that airs mornings and evenings, Robertson and his cohosts (a white woman and a black man) chat with like-minded movie stars, athletes, politicians, religious leaders, and everyday Christians. One can tune in to see singer Donna Summer, actor Charlton Heston, Attorney General Edwin Meese, or President Reagan chatting with Pat. Robertson then takes time to pray for viewers, many of whom call in for counseling. His charismatic approach includes healings and prayers for miracles. Everything from hemorrhoids to hurricanes have been successfully cured by Robertson's TV prayers. For example, when Hurricane *Gloria* was bearing down on Robertson's university and expensive television studios, Pat took to the airwaves for intervention, and sure enough, the hurricane bypassed his Virginia Beach studios.

The CBN Cable Network has risen to second place nationally since its near collapse in 1981. How? By appealing to nostalgia. Christian religious programming is now minimal, with the popular "700 Club" and a few CBN inhouse "Specials" continuing. The remainder of the programming includes a mixture of old Westerns ("Gunsmoke," "Wagontrain," and "The Rifleman"), and Hollywood sitcoms or gameshows ("The Best of Groucho," "Flipper," "Dobey Gillis," etc.). Programs are carefully selected to reflect good old American family values, including the American frontier spirit and a strong national defense. Meanwhile, more viewers are drawn into Pat Robertson's sphere of influence.

Robertson utilizes "The 700 Club" talk-show platform to call Americans back to the "good old days" and to warn about the dangers of secular humanism. While viewers are engaged in reliving the fifties and early sixties through CBN programs, Robertson provides the political and religious agenda that will re-Christianize America. He says:

> The majority of Americans are Christians, but this is not a Christian nation. You have to respect the rights of minorities. But no society can give an absolute veto power to small minorities in our midst. Six percent of our population are atheists, and you cannot give atheists a veto over the will of the majority. What I see is that the Supreme Court in the last 20 years has departed from history and our Constitution. I am worried about the encroachment of the judiciary. All I want to do is return 25 or 30 years back down the road.[5]

Critics note that CBN is getting rich on simple answers, fantasy programming, and pure nostalgia for a by gone era. CBN Program Director, Tim Robertson (Pat's son) responded to these challenges:

> I don't know that television should be just like life. Maybe television should hold up something a little bit better. These are shows that say that you can be a good person and still be a winner. You can win. That's essentially the message of Christianity. You can win.[6]

The winners are generally White American Christians (usually males) who oppose Communism. Success, wealth, strength, and happy endings are in vogue again. But what about the so-called losers, those outside these traditional categories of Christian victors? And of course, stereotypes of blacks, women, Native Americans, Jews, and Arabs, are ignored despite efforts by two generations of Americans to overcome them.

Robertson recently claimed he has received a call from God to run for President of the United States. One can also observe that over the past year he has held a series of strategic meetings around the country to galvanize support and raise funds for a possible Presidential bid. In July, 1986, he received considerable financial backing from the multi-billion dollar Hunt family, ultra-conservative Republicans from Texas. Last October (1985) he met with Chicago Democratic Boss, "Fast Eddie" Vrdolyak, leader of the white ethnic opposition to Chicago's black mayor Harold Washington. Deals can be struck in Chicago (and other urban areas) among white reactionary Democrats and an historically weak Republican Party to deliver 50-60 delegates from Chicago alone for Robertson in the March 1987 Primary.[7]

Robertson's key constituencies appear to be three-fold: first are those on the right of the Republican spectrum, who take less kindly to George Bush but tolerated Ronald Reagan; second are the white reactionaries, like Vrdolyak, who might make a deal in their city or state for a future political role in exchange for delegates; and third are the conservative and fundamentalist Christians, who subscribe to the theological presuppositions (biblical literalism, premillenialist emphasis on Armageddon, Israel, and the end-times, etc.) and the ultra-conservative political agenda of the far right.

Like Ronald Reagan, Robertson is a master of the media, particularly for these three constituencies. He knows what issues to hype and what to ignore or soften. He knows when to increase the rhetoric and how to emphasize the favorite "buzz-words." He knows when to highlight certain key aspects of his personality and what to de-emphasize. Like President Reagan, Pat Robertson knows how to make his extreme views palatable to diverse audiences. For example, he is projecting his image as a television talk-show host and businessman so as to broaden the common perception that he is only a fundamentalist evangelist.

The television access to U.S. families is buttressed by his direct mail appeals, which are skillfully mastered by conservative direct-mail wizard Richard Viguerie.

Robertson's mailing list is said to be second only to that of the Republican Party.

Over the previous two years Robertson has nurtured a new concept for fundamentalists: "The Freedom Council." It claims over 60,000 members in the U.S. alone, a staff of 50, and assets of $5.5 million. This is Robertson's political machinery. It is this grass-roots organization, composed of clergy and various leadership from churches, which he hopes will lay the ground for his political achievement. Pollster Louis Bolster has suggested that Robertson's high level "Freedom Council" could appeal to over 30 per cent of the voters in 1988.[8]

A stunning example of Robertson's political potential was the Freedom Council's work in Iowa during 1986. It brought a victory to Robertson's forces as they captured the Republican party's apparatus in Des Moines and nearby counties. The strategy was executed primarily through fundamentalist churches. The First Assembly of God and First

Federated Church of Des Moines each sent more than fifty delegates to the Republican Convention to facilitate the victory.

Pro-Robertson candidates were briefed by Freedom Council staff to "disguise" their religious and political views and to "pretend" they were concerned about economic issues. A pamphlet for Christian organizers in Des Moines told followers:

> To a degree, keep your position on issues to yourself. Come across as being interested in economic issues. Hide your strength. Don't flaunt your Christianity.[9]

These Lyndon LaRouche tactics worked in Iowa, and undoubtedly will be repeated.

Iowa was an unexpected victory for Robertson. *The Des Moines Register's* analysis of the electorate demonstrated even more so. Fifty-three percent of Iowans are mainstream Protestants (primarily Methodists and Lutherans). Twenty-five percent are Catholic with fifteen percent evangelical or fundamentalists. Therefore, Robertson's recruiting tactics in fundamentalist churches, the element of disguise, and flooding caucuses or primaries with Robertsonites can work.

However, a 1983 analysis of the Christian Right titled *The Evangelical Voter* suggests that evengelical voters constitute a total of 25-30 percent of the electorate but only one fourth of the evangelicals are fundamentalists.[10] There are a number of other indicators that show Robertson would have a difficult time gaining even a majority of the evangelical bloc. A recent straw poll by the major umbrella organization for evangelicals, The National Association of Evangelicals, showed more evangelicals favoring Congressman Jack Kemp or Senator William Armstrong of Colorado. And the influencial fundamentalist leader of the "Moral Majority," Jerry Falwell, has made public his support for Vice-President George Bush. Many evangelicals part company with Robertson's ultraconservative political agenda as well as with his charismatic and premillennialist theology. Nonetheless, Robertson's goal is to woo as many evangelicals as possible to support his candidacy.

Robertson's open endorsement of political campaigns has raised repeated accusations that he is using his television programs to destroy the principle of church and state separation. Robertson wants to Christianize the nation and its institutions, especially the Supreme Court. He says, "I think we should engage in advocacy journalism."[12] As a result, "The 700 Club " viewers see appeals to send funds for the Contra rebels, to oppose sanctions against South Africa, to increase military and financial assistance to Israel, to support strict conservative Christian appointees to the Supreme Court and much more. Moreover, Robertson has employed the conservative newspaper and Moonie think-tank *The Washington Times* to write documentaries and assist CBN's news programs. But CBN's journalistic tactics have come under severe criticism.

In 1981, Norman Lear's "People of the American Way" challenged Robertson's use of the television and won an FCC ruling. P.A.W. gained five 30 minute programs in Lcs Angeles, drawing a letter from Robertson to Norman Lear in which he reminded Lear that he [Robertson] was a former Golden Gloves boxer. He added the following threat:

> The suppression of the voice of God's servant is a terrible thing! God himself will fight for me against you—and he will win.[13]

In a more serious but less publicized case, Congressman Mervyn Dymally (D. Cal.) spoke on the floor of the House of Representatives concerning the "irresponsible journalism" of CBN. On a November 5, 1985 broadcast, CBN had accused one of the Congressman's staff of being a P.L.O. member and exercising P.L.O. influence over families of the U.S. hostages held captive in Lebanon. Dymally accused CBN of telling three lies, of being guilty of racial bigotry in its accusations against the staffer, and of jeopardizing both the life and future career of the staffer with this crass journalism. Dymally buttressed his case about the danger of such irresponsible accusations by referring to the campaign of terror then being conducted against Arab Americans. As a case in point, he recalled the murder of Palestinian American Alex Odeh in Los Angeles one month earlier, a victim of similar journalistic excesses.[14]

Robertson, like the other televangelists, will frequently become involved in U.S. foreign policy issues. His activity in this field will vary from comments made during the "700 Club," direct lobbying, or financial assistance to favorite causes. His Operation Blessing relief program, for example, hosted the commander-in-chief of the Contra forces, who are fighting to topple Nicaragua's Sandanista government. CBN, through Operation Blessing, has donated over $3 million to the Contras. CBN also works in Honduras, El Salvador, and Guatemala with retired General H.C. "Hienie" Aderholt, a contributing editor to *Soldier of Fortune* magazine.[15]

But Robertson's strongest foreign policy suite is the Middle East. Coming from a clearly premillennialist theology, Robertson and other CBN spokespersons see Israel as the key to history, with faithfulness to Israel serving as a litmus test as to how God will judge individuals and nations. Robertson sees his own success as directly linked to his support of Israel. Standing on the Mount of Olives in Jerusalem (but inside the Intercontinental Hotel) on Christmas Night 1974, Robertson recalls his vow:

> I swore a vow to the Lord that despite the opposition to Israel on many sides . . . we would stand with Israel, come what may. And that was the turning point for the entire ministry of CBN.[16]

He looks back upon Israel's birth in 1948 and the War of 1967, with Israel's military occupation of three Arab countries, as a fulfillment of Biblical prophesy. Robertson's views on events leading up to the last days parallel those of Hal Lindsay, Jerry Falwell, Mike Evans, and notably Ronald Reagan.

In a "Pat Robertson's Perspectives" newsletter he wrote:

> Jesus Christ gave us the key to modern-day events with these words: 'And Jerusalem will be trampled underfoot by the Gentiles until the times of the Gentiles be fulfilled'(Luke 21:24). Put another way, Jesus was saying that the termination of Gentile spiritual privilege and the power that results from it would take place when the Jews took control of Jerusalem . . . . June, 1967, therefore, becomes the prophetic benchmark for the rapid disintegration of Gentile world power. Consider these events after 1967: a humiliating U.S. loss in Vietnam, the first military loss in our history; virulent worldwide inflation, the fall of the dollar as the great world currency; the worldwide oil crisis; Communist advances throughout Africa; upheaval in Iran; a plague of abortion, homosexuality, occultism, and pornography, . . . Russian troops and planes in Cuba; the Afghan invasion; impending worldwide depression; potential Middle East war or even World War III.[17]

Thus, the Israeli capture of Jerusalem and occupation of the West Bank and Gaza were signs of Israel's rise to power, and the decline of Europe and the United States. The dual themes of America's decline, due to immorality and military weakness, coupled with Israel's rise, have parallel's in the earliest Christian premillennialist and Christian Zionist thinkers. Thus both a theological assumption (Israel's rise to power and Jesus' Second Coming) and political themes (anti-secular humanism or modernism, anti-Communism, and strong national militarism) converge in the Middle East, anticipating the Armageddon showdown.

In 1982, with Israel's invasion of Lebanon, Robertson predicted in his newsletter a Soviet attack on Israel before the end of the year. He sensed a favorite premillennialist passage, Ezekiel 38-39 (Gog and Magog), was coming to pass. In the early stages of Israel's assault on Lebanon and Palestinian population centers, Robertson called upon his viewers to pray and take action to allow President Reagan to encourage Israel to go further in its invasion.[18]

Robertson believes that a nuclear Armageddon is inevitable, and will probably occur as the result of a super power confrontation in the Middle East. When the nuclear showdown begins, Jesus Christ will return. Conveniently, the true believers will be translated out of history in what premillennialists call "The Rapture." After Jesus' return, Israel's opponents will be defeated and a thousand year reign of peace established, with Jesus' headquarters in Israel. The exact site of Jesus' base is a matter of speculation but the rebuilt Third Temple is probable.

Robertson's apocalyptic views of history and the Bible color his foreign policy with a sense of theological determinism. His rhetoric on these matters is slightly less dogmatic in 1986 than it was three or four years ago, but the basic elements remain the same. He summarized his views on these matters in early 1986:

> I have felt that one day the Soviets or their satellites will invade Israel. I do not think the U.S. is going to go to war with the Soviets over Israel. But we might be drawn into something. This is the most volatile area in the whole world and if you read the Bible, it seems to be considered the center of the earth. If something were to happen, of course the U.S. would come down on the side of the Israelis.[19]

A Robertson presidency will parallel, if not accelerate the United State's economic and military support of Israel, now over $14 million per day.

Robertson's business and personal co-operation with Israel has been strong over the years. CBN has donated generously to the United Jewish Appeal and other Zionist charities, in addition to CBN's relief efforts in Israel. In exchange, Israel has been good to Robertson, supporting and protecting his television station in southern Lebanon, even though Israel's Knesset passed a law forbidding evangelism. Robertson explains:

> They realize that our purpose is to bring peace to the Middle East. . . . [The station is] going to help usher in the Second Coming of Christ.[20]

Does Robertson have any compassion or sense of justice toward the 4.5 million Palestinians, half of whom suffer directly from Israel's military occupation and Iron Fist reign? Robertson has little to say about justice and human rights for the Palestinians, focusing more on Israel's security needs and his larger Armageddon scenario. He recently stated:

> Israel has to live within secure borders. The U.S. can't force Israel to give up what Prime Minister Begin called Judea and Samaria. The only intelligent solution would be a confederation of an Arab entity on the West Bank within Israeli parameters. That entity would not be an independent Palestinian state. It would be allied with Israel.[21]

Thus Robertson subscribes to a Jewish fundamentalist, or Likud, scheme, which offers the Palestinians no more than prolonged misery and subservience.

Despite this overwhelming commitment to Israel and the goals of revisionist Zionism, many jews are suspicious of Robertson's oft-stated views on evangelism of the Jews. After CBN acquired Channel 12, The Star of Hope television channel in southern Lebanon, Robertson drafted a seven page fundraising letter that mentioned his plan to use television to convert the peoples of the Middle East to fundamentalist Christianity. Robertson wrote:

> God's Holy Spirit is about to be poured out on the Holy Land. Miracles are about to abound. God's chosen ones are about to see more and more of the direct revelation of Jesus Christ.[22]

Nevertheless, at this stage of Israeli-U.S. relations, the State of Israel is more than willing to shelve its ban on evangelism and keep its fundamentalist Rabbis under-wrap in order to glean the multiple blessings of Robertson's support of Zionism in North America, and throughout the world.

The Hebrew prophets, from Samuel and Elijah to Isaiah and Jeremiah, stood outside the corridors of power to challenge Israel and Judah to walk faithfully in God's path. The prophets were consistently persecuted and maligned because of their opposition to Israel's political leaders. Their oracles often predicted judgment and doom upon the Kings and Queens, who the prophets viewed as opposing the will of God. The prophet always kept a calculated distance from the trappings of royalty so as to maintain their strict independence and radical dependence upon God alone.

Clearly, Pat Robertson's understanding of the prophetic role is different. He believes that God has called him to the Oval Office itself. As the Chief Executive of the United States, Pat Robertson will be able to guide America into the latter days of history.

NOTES

1. *Psychology Today* (April, 1983), p. 21.
2. George Will, "Pat Robertson's Mustard Seed," *Newsweek* (March 3, 1986), p. 72.
3. "40% of Viewers Watch TV Preachers," *Washington Post* (October 25, 1985), p. A-1.
4. Two recent studies are Tod A. Baker, Robert P. Steed, and Lawrence Moreland, *Religion and Politics in the South* (New York: Prager Publishing, 1984), and James Davison Hunter, *American Evangelicalism* (New Brunswick, New Jersey: Rutgers Univ. Press, 1983).
5. Pat Aufderheide, "Pat Robertson," *On Cable* (May 1985), p. 18.
6. James Traub, "CBN Counts Its Blessings," *Channels of Communication* (May/June, 1985), p. 31.
7. James Wall, Editorial in *Christian Century* (Oct. 23, 1985), p. 939.
8. William Saletan, "Teflon Telepreacher," *The New Republic* (Jan. 20, 1986), p. 10.
9. Albert J. Menendez, "Righter Than Thou," *Church and State* (July/August, 1986), p. 13.
10. Saletan, p. 10.
11. Jon Margolis, "Evangelicals Worry GOP Regulars," *Chicago Tribune* (June 18, 1986) A-1.
12. Pat Aufderheide, "The Next Voice You Hear," *The Progressive* (Sept., 1985), p. 35.
13. Ibid., p. 36.
14. "Irresponsible Journalism," *Congressional Record* (Nov. 12, 1985), H-10014-16.
15. Vicki Kemper, "In the Name of Relief," *Sojourners* (Oct., 1985), pp. 12-16.
16. Letter from Robertson to CBN Friends, April, 1982, p. 4.
17. "Special Issue: Prophetic Insights for the Decade of Destiny," *Pat Robertson's Perspectives* (February/March, 1980), CBN, Virginia Beach, VA, p. 2.
18. Aufderheide, op. cit., p. 36.
19. *Time Magazine* (Feb. 17, 1986), p. 66.
20. Aufderheide, op. cit., p. 36.
21. "Interview," *Christianity Today* (Jan. 17, 1986), p. 35.
22. Quoted in Lawrence Epstein, *Zion's Call* (New York: Univ. Press of America, 1984), p. 134.

Modern Israel and Biblical Prophecies

BY BERT DE VRIES, PH.D.

The belief that the creation of the state of Israel in 1947 was the fulfillment of the biblical prophecies is currently very popular among American Christians. This belief is readily accepted by many Christians who assume that the current Jewish possession of the land is merely a recent phase in the long confrontation between Isaac and Ishmael, in which God is clealry on the side of Isaac who received the inheritance so long ago. Moreover, this belief has been one of the central doctrines in the theology of dispensationalism.[1] In this theological system it is held that the signs of the times preparing the faithful for the second coming of Christ are clearly spelled out in Scripture, and that they can be identified with current events with the confidence of an eyewitness news reporter. In this system the return of Israel is one of the essential end-time signs. And its believed realization in the state of Israel is one of the great assurances that Jesus is coming soon.

This view of biblical prophecy has had an influence among numerous Christians who are not dispensationalists. Perhaps this is due to the lasting popularity of the *Scofield Reference Bible,* but certainly it is due to the simple solution it offers to complex and often frightening current events. The notion that God's prophets appear to be more reliable commentators on current events than members of the journalistic profession is certainly appealing to many. (Often when I speak on the Arab-Israeli conflict I see numerous members of the audience holding Bibles rather protectively. Is this their symbolic message to me that anything I have to say about current events will fade to irrelevance in the light of the words of the prophets?)

The dispensational view of the state of Israel has gained renewed popularity among American Christians because it has been a cornerstone in the evangelism of popular television preachers such as Jerry Falwell. Falwell makes no bones about the fact that God's promises to Abraham in Genesis 12, 15, and 17 apply directly to modern Israel; this includes applying the curse of Genesis 12:3 to Arabs and whoever else may be critical of Israel. Because of his status as leader of the Moral Majority, Israeli officials have treated him as a statesman on his numerous visits to Israel. They recognize that his brand of Christian Zionism is currently the major source of American popular support for the U.S. government's pro-Israeli policies.

The above article is reprinted with permission from the author. It originally appeared in *Occasional Papers from Calvin College*, vol. 4, No.1, February, 1986. Bert De Vries, Ph.D., is Professor of History at Calvin College.

How is this confident claim to be dealt with? Space does not permit an exegetical analysis of each passage that refers to the restoration of Israel. For thoughtful treatment of these passages from a Reformed point of view I recommend the following books: Dewey M. Beegle, *Prophecy and Prediction* (Ann Arbor: Pryor Pettengill, 1978); Colin Chapman, *Whose Promised Land?* (Ann Arbor: Lion Publishing Corporation, 1983); Anthony A. Hoekema, *The Bible and the Future* (Grand Rapids: William B. Erdmans Publishing Company, 1979). What I can do here is make some generalizations about the theological and practical weaknesses of this view of prophecy.[2]

THEOLOGICAL WEAKNESSES

The direct identification of biblical prophecies with modern Israel pulls these passages out of context and simplistically ignores both more obvious and more complex alternative interpretations. At least the following possibilities for interpreting these prophetic passages are ignored:

1. **Fulfillment of prophecies of the return in the Old Testament**. When Ezekiel, for example, addressed his prophecies to the Israelites in captivity in Babylon, they were fulfilled in the return to Palestine in the sixth century B.C. It should be noted, moreover, that the prophets spoke in their own specific historical context. They did not simply go around making predictions of events 2500 years in the future. Rather, they were commissioned by God to comment on the behavior of their own contemporaries. Instead of journalists of events in the twentieth century, they were God's commentators on the political, social, and religious events of their own times. The meaning of the prophecies in their contemporary setting is often simply ignored in the enthusiastic quotation of "proof-texts" that appear to apply to modern Israel.

2. **Spiritual conversion as a condition for fulfillment**. God's promises for Israel were always given in a covenant context. The promise of the land to Abraham's seed is accompanied with the condition: "Walk before me, and be thou perfect" (Gen. 17:16). This makes all subsequent prophetic announcements to Israel conditional. The remnant, those to whom God is promising return and restoration, is made up of those who have remained faithful and those who have repented. Thus, prophecies of return and restoration cannot be divorced from prophecies of spiritual conversion. In fact this conversion may be the major message of the restoration promise of which the physical return is merely a symbolic component. Ezekiel says in the context of the famous vision of the dry bones (37:1-14): "Neither will they defile themselves any more with their idols . . . , but I will save them out of all their dwelling places wherein they have sinned, and will cleanse them: so shall they be my people and I will be their God" (Ezek. 37:23).

3. **The universal emphasis of prophecy**. The direction of prophetic revelation in the Old Testament is from particular to universal. Its movement is from a particular man, Abraham, to a particular people, Israel, to all nations. Already at the dedication of Solomon's temple it is made clear that God is not just a tribal God for whom the temple will be a dwelling place among Israel. The temple is to be the place in which both Israelite and foreigner can address God who dwells in heaven.

"But will God in very deed dwell on the earth? Behold, heaven and the heavens cannot contain thee; how much less this house that I have builded!" (I Kings 8:43). The message of the later prophets includes the proclamation that the nation of Israel no longer has any special status: "Are ye not as the children of the Ethiopians unto me, O children of Israel?

saith Jehovah. Have I not brought up Israel out of the land of Egypt, and the Philistines from Caphtor, and the Syrians from Kir?'' (Amos 9:7).

The according of special status to modern Israel ignores the revelational movement from particular to universal; in fact, it reverses it. It is as though we are back to Joshua at the Jordan River. Does Canaan have to be conquered again?

4. **The fulfillment of Old Testament prophecy in the New Testament**. The universalism of the Old Testament prophets has its culmination in the New Testament. Citizenship in the nation of Israel as a territorial, earthly kingdom is replaced by citizenship in the Kingdom of God, a spiritual realm whose members are chosen not on the basis of nationality but on the basis of their conversion in Christ. The focus of God's redemption is transferred from Israel to a new people made up of both Jewish and Gentile disciples of Christ. Whatever special status Paul attributes to Israel and the Jew has to be considered in the light of his major emphasis: special status is based on election by God, not on a distinction between Israel and the Gentiles.[3]

The direct application of Old Testament prophecies to modern Israel de-emphasizes the role of Christ in God's plan. This perhaps explains why dispensationalists are so fond of talking of God's plan for the present in terms of Old Testament-style clashes of nations. If you ignore the incarnation, Canaan may in fact have to be conquered again.

5. **The literal fulfillment of prophecy in modern history**. To claim that the literal fulfillment of prophecy is impossible would be as presumptuous as to assume that it is the only approach to prophecy.The denial that biblical prophecy is being fulfilled in contemporary history comes close to denying that God is involved in modern history. Even then, the question still remains: Is the Christian able to identify modern events with biblical prophetic predictions?

It should be remembered that the return of Israel is seen in the dispensational scheme as one of the signs that enables one to figure out when the second coming of Christ will be. However, Jesus himself warned that the attempt to predict this return is a fruitless and dangerous business: "Therefore, be ye also ready; for in an hour that ye think not the Son of man cometh'' (Matt. 24:44). "Then if any man shall say unto you, lo, here is the Christ, or here; believe it not. For there shall arise false Christs, and false prophets, and shall show great signs and wonders; so as to lead astray, if possible, even the elect'' (Matt. 24:23-24).

PRACTICAL WEAKNESSES

The conviction that modern Israel is one of the signs of the times, a step in God's end-time table, may trap the Christian into some less-than-Christian practices:

1. **It leads to use of the Bible as a crystal ball**. The belief that Israel is a clear step in God's scheme has given many Christians the confidence that they can chart the still-to-be-fulfilled signs and thus trace the divine blueprint into the millennium. This use of the Bible to predict the future gives a sense of certainty and security in an age that otherwise seems to offer only the opposite. However, in the light of the passages just quoted this may in fact be a serious abuse of the Bible, because it tempts the believer to put his faith in the blueprint rather than in God himself.

2. **It forces God into a pattern**. Frequently people like Falwell who see modern Israel as prophecy come true believe strongly that God is on the side of Israel in the Middle East political struggle. This seems to me to come very close to the Crusader and Muslim militants' belief that God marched into battle with them . Thus God becomes the servant

of geo-politics rather the the Lord of history. And the Christian, armed with his end-time chart, can shout: "God, this is what you're supposed to do next!" No mere man may make the arrogant claim that he knows the mind of God, of course, for he could do so only by playing the role of God himself.

3. **It excuses the state of Israel from the modern international code of proper and just behavior**. The assumption is that if God is on the side of Israel and if Israel is prophecy come true, God must condone Israel's behavior. Thus Israel's ignoring of U.N. decrees, illegal settlements of the Occupied Territories, and aggression into Lebanon need not be judged by the same standards by which ordinary nations are judged. The fact is, of course, that if Israel were God's specially chosen nation, the mark of that would not be a license to break international rules, but a mandate to be God's servants. Chosenness means awesome responsibility, not frivolous privilege.

4. **It makes it unnecessary to pay attention to the actual events of current history**. If one is convinced that an event was predetermined by biblical prophecy, one need not understand what is actually happening in the present. The result is a remarkable lack of interest in the details of the Arab-Israeli Conflict and an almost deliberate ignoring of the suffering experienced by so many people in the Middle East as a result of that conflict. People who assume that the Israelis have the right to do as they please, will also assume that the Palestinians deserve what they get, no matter what the specifics of the events are. The product of this is a decided lack of a sense of compassion for people in the conflict. This neglect of present history goes counter to Christian notions of mercy and love. Palestinians and others ought to be recipients of God's good news rather than mere victims of supra-historical forces. No matter what God has in mind for human beings, his children have no choice but to treat them as fellow creatures. That includes treating them according to how they act, not who they are. In that Palestinian Arabs and Israeli Jews are equal.

NOTES

1. For the definitive treatment of the historical origins of dispensationalism see George Marsden, *Fundamentalism and American Culture* (New York: Oxford University Press, 1980).

2. What follows is a reworking of Bert De Vries, "'His Land' and Prophecy," *The Reformed Journal* (Nov. 1971), 10-13.

3. For an interpretation of Romans 9-11 see Anthony A. Hoekema, *The Bible and the Future* (Grand Rapids: Erdmans Publishing Co., 1979), 139-147.

A Palestinian Christian Response: An Interview with Jonathan Kuttab

BY GRACE HALSELL

To find out why followers of Christ raise millions of dollars for Zionists, I went to Jonathan Kuttab, a Palestinian Christian who gave up a successful law practice in the United States to return to his native land, where he now serves as attorney and director of Law in the Service of Man, a West Bank affiliate of the International Commission of Jurists. After introductions, I asked Kuttab how he interprets the hearts and minds of American Christians who travel to the land of Christ and see stone monuments, but fail to see the native people.

"There is a Christian folk religion, a mythology of Israel and prophecy and it has nothing to do with biblical Christianity. This folk religion is not demanding, nor a moral or highly ethical religion. It is a macho religion based on a 'worship' of the small, ultra-powerful Israel, which is not a sissy. Their God is a cross between Superman and Star Wars, who zaps here and there with fiery, swift sword and destroys all the enemies. And that is appealing. He is proof for those of weak faith that the Bible is still true and alive. It's almost as if Joshua is here in the daily newspaper.

"This Christian Zionism has nothing to do with morality, nothing to do with ethics or wrestling with the real, serious problem," Kuttab continues. "It has nothing to do with the humanity of the other side. The American right-wing Christians have a kind of God with whom the common man can identify. Their leaders tell them to support Israel. So, what is three billion dollars in the U.S. budget? The average American does not even know about it. And as a Christian Zionist, you are on the right side, the 'good' side, the successful winning side. Their religion feeds into all the racism about Orientals generally, and all the stereotypes about Muslims and Arabs. So on a psychological level, it is a very understandable phenomenon. It has nothing to do with Christianity, of course. But it is a mythology."

How much of the Christian Zionism, I ask Kuttab, is tied in with big politics and big money? "Here in Jerusalem, the so-called Christian Embassy is very much tied in with big power, big money and the power structure. The decision to open the Christian Embassy in Jerusalem was made at the highest Israeli level — involving then Prime Minister Begin. The decision obviously was political. When the Christian Embassy was started, they announced seven goals, six clearly political. The seventh was to preach about Christ to the Jews. But under some pressure, they dropped the seventh one. And now they only have the six goals, all involving a closer political alliance with the Zionists. So to me this means that the Christian aspect, if they had any, was merely second to the political aspects.

"The Christians give the Israelis carte blanche," Kuttab continues. "They encourage them in their refusal to recognize the Palestinians, in their refusal to withdraw from the West Bank and make compromises, and become peacemakers. In fact, they provide them with an incentive to expand and take more and oppress more because God is on their side and Uncle Sam is willing to foot the bill. And so the Israelis know that good, solid blue-blooded Christians are with them all the way, regardless of what they do morally or ethically or regardless of what the rest of the world thinks. And regardless of how oppressive they become, they know the American Christians are with them and America is willing to pay; America is willing to give them weapons and America is willing to vote with them in the United Nations.

"So the Christians are part of the problem. And they are not doing Israel a favor, either. There is a lot of patronizing and a lot of anti-Semitism involved in this kind of support. The Christians are saying, quietly, to each other, 'And the Jews can go to Israel and stay *there.*' They believe that God is going to gather all the Jews in Palestine and then the unspoken end of the sentence is 'So they can all be killed in Armageddon...' That is the part of the sentence that is not always emphasized. So, despite their short-term support of Zionism, the Christians who come here often harbor a lot of anti-Semitism. In fact precisely because of these Christian's anti-Semitism, they go all out for Israel. They do this because they are afraid of being charged with anti-Semitism. In his heart the evangelical or fundamentalist Christian may wish to eradicate Judaism by the conversion of all Jews. For his own short term goal, he forgets this and 'loves' Israel — while at the same time he may not like the Jews."

(Reprinted with permission from *The Link,* Americans for M.E. Understanding. Grace Halsell is a free-lance writer living in Washington, D.C. and is author of *Soul Sister* and *Journey to Jerusalem.*)

They Must Go . . . In The Name of The Bible: Rabbi Meir Kahane's "Apartheid" Zionism

BY GOODMAN SMITH

Meir Kahane's Zionism is clear and straightforward. He does not try to apologize for it, or to sugar-coat it with claims of liberalism, humanism, and democratic ideals as do most other brands of Zionism. It is unashamedly and unequivocally one-sided, drawn with bold monochrome lines, a picture of crude, frank, national egocentrism dressed in priestly robes. It starts with the basic premise of Zionism which is that the Jews are different from other people: a distinction that can be accommodated and nourished only in a distinct piece of land: Palestine. Kahane believes that Israel's history, politics and morals are not to be judged except by its own standards. These standards are not man-made, they are of divine origin, a Torah. As a Jewish state, Israel is a country for the Jews and the Jews only, God-ordained and destined for a "holy mission." Non-Jews (in small numbers) could live in Israel only as "resident-strangers" who could not have any of the rights or duties of the Jews. (More on resident-strangers below).

Secular and humanist Zionists, who, by their profession of Zionism assert their belief in the special distinction of the Jews, the "territorial imperative" in Palestine, and the Jewish character of the state of Israel, may still call for some accommodation with the Arabs. Their Zionism, as such, is a little pregnant with humanism![1]

In Israel, Kahane's brand of ultra-nationalistic Zionism is challenging Labor, and all liberal Zionists everywhere, to answer a simple question: If the Arabs in Israel became a majority, will Israel remain a Jewish State? Is Israel ready to give up its "rightful" heritage of Judea and Samaria? And if not, what should it do about the Arabs there who might, one day, threaten the Jewish character of the state? Israel's ruling parties do not have a straight answer to these questions, at least an answer they can openly espouse.

But Meir Kahane does. He possesses none of the scruples of secular-humanist Zionists. He does not give a thought to the accusation that Zionism is racism, an accusation that troubles liberal Zionists very much. His Zionism is blatantly racist, because, he maintains, it ought to be so by Torah principles and commandments. He makes that clear in his book, *THEY MUST GO,* (Grosset and Dunlap, New York, 1981). After presenting his case with political, economic, and historical arguments, he summons at the end the authority of the Bible and the Rabbinical literature explaining and expounding on the scripture to advance and preach his brand of Zionism. His Zionism is—as he put it—a *Torah* Zionism, and the nation Israel, is a *Torah* community, setting it apart from, and above all nations, above history, above ethics. This "*uber alles*" mentality rests squarely on the will of the "L-rd G-d of Israel."

The concluding chapter in his book titled "There is a G-d in Israel" reveals with great emphasis the biblical and Talmudic anchor of Kahane's belief in Israel's "apartheid" nature. The uniqueness of the Jew and of Israel is paramount in his understanding of the question of the Arabs in Israel. His recommendations for action against the Arabs rest on his belief, based on Torah, that Israel's uniqueness requires it to be a purely Jewish nation. Therefore, he recommends the eviction of all Arabs from Israel, in defiance of any legal, political, or moral forces. If God is behind the plan, why should Israel fear any power? Quoting Jeremiah 30:11: "Though I put an end to all the nations among whom thou art scattered, but I will never put an end to thee," he brazenly concludes:[2]

> Israel is indestructible. It is unique, it is holy, it is the Chosen of the L-rd; it has a reason for being. Its national uniqueness is built on an idea, on an ideology, that it alone has. That is, indeed, reason to be different. The Jew is selected and obligated to be a religio-nation, commanded to obey the laws and follow the path of Torah . . . The Jew is commanded to create for himself a holy nation and that can only be done free of others, separate, different, apart. That is why the unique Jewish nation, chosen for holiness and a unique destiny, was given a land for itself: so that it might create a unique, holy society that would be a light unto the nations who would see its example and model.

Kahane's idea of Israel's mission to the world, to be a model and a light unto the nations is shared by almost all shades of Zionists, even the most liberal. This is, so to speak, the Jewish version of the "White Man's Burden," or the "mission civiliatrice" of European colonialists. The humanist-philosopher Zionist, Martin Buber, enthusiastically preached the same idea of the consecration of the Land and the People for "a divine mission." In his famous letter to Mahatma Gandhi he states: "We could not and cannot renounce the Jewish claim [to Palestine]; something even higher than the life of our people is bound up with this land, namely its work, its divine mission."[3]

The uniqueness of the Jew is linked to the uniqueness of the Jewish nation (Israel), and this in turn is mystically linked to a unique piece of land (Palestine). All this mystifying linkage is to fulfill a universal mission, a religious "new order." Israel is to be a model to the nations. Kahane does not say whether this role implies that all nations should consider themselves unique and chosen by their "L-rd." The paradox in this statement eludes the outspoken Rabbi. This is why Kahane's conscience is clear, for he is doing the bidding of his G-d, and is in no need for mere human logic. His call for the forceful eviction of all Arabs from the Land of Israel, meaning, of course, all Palestine and beyond, is a necessary step for the creation of the "Model Israel" to be the "light of the nations." This expulsion is based on a previous biblical model:

> The L-rd, Creator and Proprietor of the world—all the lands are his. He took that which was His from the Canaanites and gave it to His Chosen People Israel. "And He gave them the lands of the nations and they inherited the lands of the people, so that they would observe His statutes and guard His laws . . . " (Psalms 105:44-45). The right of the Jewish people to the land is not based on human favors or historical residence. It is a title granted by the Builder and Owner. Clearly, it was not taken from one set of nations in order that others share it with the Jews. The land was given to serve the Jewish people so that they have a distinct, separate place in which to fulfill their obligation. There can be no others who freely live there, let alone share sovereignty and ownership. To allow such a thing is to destroy and put an end to that unique Torah society for which the Land of Israel was given to the Jews.

Kahane does not have to resort to falsification of history or to convoluted logic to avoid a feeling of guilt toward the eviction and dispossession of the Palestinians. He does not indulge in doublespeak by saying two rights are in conflict in Palestine, or falsify documents to prove the Palestinians never lived in Palestine, or assert that the Palestinians do not exist. He did not even make use of the early Zionist guilt-evading claim of "a land without people for a people without land." His total and categorical belief that the Land of Israel has to be "redeemed" no matter who or what stands in the way, is refreshingly bullish and frank.

To bring about this Torah society, the apartness and uniqueness of the Jewish people have to be preserved in the Land that God had set for this sublime undertaking. The redemption of the land is, as such, a religious obligation:

> The land was given as a reward, as a blessing. But it is more, much more, than that. The people of Israel have more than a *right* to the land; they have an *obligation.* "For you shall pass over the Jordan to go in to possess the Land which the L-rd your G-d gives you, and you shall possess it and dwell therein" (Deuteronomy 11:31).

It is quite clear that the possession of the land (and the expulsion of the indigenous inhabitants therein) is not a political or economic decision of a group of people, but a direct order from the Lord Himself. It is for His sake, and for the sake of His plan for the ages, that Israel is to be created and maintained. This can occur (mysteriously) nowhere on earth except in a unique land which is also assigned by the Divine. The holy mission of Israel is divinely bound by this particular land. None other is acceptable to the Lord:

> A unique people given, uniquely, a *particular* land Unlike all the other faiths that are not limited to one special country, the Jew is given a particular land and commanded to live there. And for a reason, as Moses explains: "Behold, I have taught you statutes and judgments, even as the L-rd, my G-d, commanded me, *that you shall do so in the Land whither you go to possess it"* (Deuteronomy 4:5) (Kahane's emphasis).

Kahane defines the borders of this unique land by quoting Torah:

> Eretz Yisrael. "Unto thy seed have I given this land from the river of Egypt unto the great river, the River Euphrates" (Genesis 15:18).

We can safely assume that Kahane's long term plans include the expulsion of the Arabs of all Syria, including Jordan and Lebanon. The L-rd's blueprint for the "Holy Model Nation" will have to be complete. Kahane reemphasizes his call for the expulsion of the Palestinians by citing another biblical model:

> So basic and important is this concept [of not sharing the Holy Land with non-Jews] that as the Jews prepared to cross the Jordan into the land of Israel, as the waters rose to enormous heights and the Children of Israel rapidly crossed to the other side, as they were in the middle of now-dry riverbed, suddenly Joshua paused and spoke to them. What was so vital that could not wait until they had crossed safely to the other side? . . . While still in the Jordan, Joshua said to them: "Know why you are crossing the Jordan! In order that you drive out the inhabitants of the Land from before you as it is written" (Numbers 33:52). "And you shall drive out all the inhabitants of the land from before you." "If you do this—it shall be good. If not—the waters shall come and inundate me and you." (Talmud, Sota 34a).

Possessing the land and driving out the goyim are equally essential. Conquest of the land without a total "clean-up" of all the unclean, non-Jewish residents, may bring on the wrath of God, the destruction of Israel, and the aborting of the divine mission. This is a religious obligation placed on the chosen to fulfill their mission of redemption.

Again and again Kahane asserts that this religious obligation to keep the Land of Israel goyim-free comes directly from the Torah. It is a direct order that can be ignored only at the risk of losing the favor of the Lord. It is, therefore, an act of piety, of worship.

> And as the Torah clearly commanded: "And you shall drive out all the inhabitants of the land from before you . . . But if you will not drive out the inhabitants of the land from before you, then it shall come to pass that those which you let remain of them, shall be thorns in your eyes and thistles in your sides and shall torment you in the land wherein you dwell. And it shall be that I will do to you as I thought to do to them (Numbers 33:52-56).

The example of previous Jewish experiments in setting up a state in the Land of Canaan is testimony to the divine imperative of "driving out the goyim of the land, " as a requirement for survival and God's blessings. Kahane summons the authority of the Talmud and other Rabbinical authoities commenting on the verse above:

> The biblical commentators are explicit: "And you shall drive out the inhabitants and then you shall inherit it, you will be able to exist in it. And if you do not, you will not be able to exist in it" (Rashi—Rabbi Shlomo Yitzchaki).
>
> "When you shall eliminate the inhabitants of the land, then you shall be privileged to inherit the land and pass it down to your children. But if you do not eliminate them, even though you will conquer the land you will not be privileged to hand it down to your children" (Sforno—Rabbi Ovadiah ben Yaakov).

The dispossession and elimination of the goyim of the land must include not only the land actually conquered, but the land which is promised but not yet conquered:

> " . . . The verse speaks of others aside from the seven Canaanite nations . . . Not only will they hold that part of the land that you did not possess, but even concerning that part which you did possess and settle in—they will distress you and say: Rise and get out . . . " (Ohr Ha'Chayimn—Rabbi Chaim ben Atar).

The details of this policy of Israel toward the non-Jewish inhabitants of the"Land" is spelled out in the Torah and the Rabbinical commentaries. We see here an added element in this policy of preserving the uniqueness of Israel, one that looks, at least to Kahane, as a very reasonable one. We are told that foreigners *may* live within the borders of the Jewish State, but with conditions. A choice is magnanimously offered to these wretched people before they are put on the butcher block:

> And so, the Talmud tells us: "Joshua sent three messages to the inhabitants [of Canaan]. He who wishes to evacuate—let him evacuate; who wishes to make peace—let him make peace; to make war—let him make war" (Va-Yikra Rabah 17).
>
> The choices are given. Either leave, or prepare for war—or make peace. The choice of "making peace" is explained by the rabbis as involving three things. To begin with, the non-Jew must agree to adopt the seven basic Noahide laws, which include prohibitions against idolatry, blasphemy, immorality, bloodshed, robbery, eating flesh cut from a living animal, and a positive action—adherence to social laws. Once he has done this, he has the status of a resident

> stranger *(ger toshav)* who is allowed to live in Eretz Yisrael (Talmud, Avoda Zara 64b), *if he also accepts the condition to tribute and servitude.* (It should be noted that the use of the word *ger*, [''stranger''] in the Torah refers invariably not to the non-Jewish stranger, but to the convert to Judaism). (Kahane's emphasis).

The ''privilege'' of living in the land of Israel, even for those who convert to Judaism, but who are not born of Jewish mothers, has a heavy price: tribute and servitude. For to the heathens (the Canaanites of old) elimination or slavery are the only choices given to them by the Torah: ''Cursed be Canaan, slave of slaves shall he be to his brothers . . . Blessed by the Lord my God is Shem; and let Canaan be his slave.'' (Genesis 9:25-26). This leaves no choice to the non-Jewish Muslim and Christian Arabs of Palestine but to move out.

Rabbinical writings, quoted by Kahane, elaborate on the policies of the Torah Community towards the resident strangers in the Land of Israel. This policy is based on the biblical commandment in Deuteronomy 20:10 ff: ''When you draw near to a city to fight against it, offer terms of peace to it. And if its answer to you is peace and it opens to you then all the people who are found in it shall do forced labor for you and shall serve you.'' (Revised Standard Version). Kahane's quote reads, ''They will be (sic) tribute and shall serve you.'' Maimonides, the most famous Jewish Rabbi and scholar of the Jewish ''Golden Age'' under Islam, explains in detail the role of the stranger in the land of Israel. Kahane writes:

> Maimonides (Hilchot Mlachim 6:11) declares: ''If they make peace and accept the seven Noahide laws we do not kill them for they are tributary. If they agreed to pay tribute but do not accept servitude or accepted servitude but not tribute we do not acquiesce until they have accepted both. And servitude means that they shall be humble and low and not raise their head in Israel. Rather they shall be subjects under us and not be appointed to any position over Jews ever.''

The Torah, as explained by Maimonides, seems to have a great effect on today's policies of Israel towards the Palestinians, as far as servitude, tribute, and humiliation are concerned. But Rabbi Kahane remains critical of the government of Israel's policies because he thinks these measures are not applied strictly enough, conclusively enough, and religiously enough. He does not separate, as far as this problem goes, between secular and religious laws:

> Far better than foolish humans did the Almighty understand the dangers inherent in allowing a people that believed the land belonged to it to be given free and unfettered residence, let alone ownership, proprietorship, citizenship. What more natural thing than to ask to regain what it believed to be rightly its own land? And this over and above the need to create a *unique* and distinctly separate Torah culture that will shape the Jewish people into a holy nation. That ''uniqueness'' can be guaranteed only by the non-Jew's having no sovereignty, ownership, or citizenship in the state that could allow him to shape its destiny and character.

The great Maimonides (and his comments on Torah) is summoned again to support the Rabbi:

> And so, concerning any non-Jew, Maimonides says: ''Thou shalt not place over thyself a stranger who is not of your brethren'' (Deuteronomy 17:15). Not only a king, but the prohibition is for any authority in Israel. Not an officer in the armed forces . . . not even a public official in charge of the

> distribution of water to the fields. And there is no need to mention that a judge or chieftain shall only be from the people of Israel . . . Any authority that you appoint shall only be from the midst of thy people. (Hilchot Mlachim 1:4)

Kahane's conditions for the strangers living in Israel go beyond humiliation, servitude, and tribute. He wants them to believe in their inferiority, and to profess that lowly status as an article of faith:

> The purpose is clear. The non-Jew has no share in the Land of Israel. He has no ownership, citizenship, or destiny in it. The non-Jew who wishes to live in Israel must accept basic human obligations. Then he may live in Israel as a *resident stranger*, but never as one who can hold any public office that will give him dominion over a Jew or a share in the authority of the country. Accepting these conditions, he admits that the land is not his, and therefore he may live in Israel quietly, separately observing his own private life, with all religious, economic, social and cultural rights. Refusing this, he cannot remain.
>
> This is Torah. This is *Jewishness.* Not the dishonest pseudo-"Judaism" chanted by the liberal secularists who pick and choose what "Judaism" finds favor in their eyes and who reject what their own gentilized concepts find unacceptable . . .

What about international pressure on Israel if this policy of racism and obtuse discrimination is applied? Kahane's boldness, even brashness, in asserting the rights of the Jews to possess the land and to drive the goyim out, is a result of his firm belief that God is behind the plan. God fights for Israel, therefore Israel should defy the powers of the world, for it is indestructible:

> And if this is not only the right of Jews but their obligation, what do we fear? Why do the Jews tremble and quake before the threat of the nations? Is there no longer a G-d in Israel? Have we so lost our bearings that we do not understand the ordained historical role of the State of Israel, a role that ensures that it can never be destroyed and that no further exile from it is possible? Why is it that we do not comprehend that *it is precisely our refusal to deal with the Arabs according to halakic obligation that will bring down on our heads terrible sufferings, whereas our courage in removing them will be one of the major factors in the hurrying of the final redemption?* (Kahane's emphasis).

It is obvious that Kahane's *final redemption* is linked by necessity to the *final solution* of the "Arab question." The Arabs are the definite obstacle to the final redemption and to the fulfillment of God's plan for the world. On this point, there is a meeting of minds between this brand of Zionism and Fundamentalist Christian Zionism. The two differ on the goal. To the Torah Zionist, it is the establishment of the State of Israel where all the Jews will be ingathered and the State will become a model for the world. To Christian Zionists, this is only a prelude and prerequisite to the Second Coming of the Lord Jesus and the establishment of the millenium. While the difference seems irreconcilable as far as the final goal is concerned, the two groups meet on the near and intermediate course of events, which is the building of the State of Israel and the continuing "ingathering" of the Jews in it. Both parties are totally convinced of the divine nature of this venture.

Kahane's model of the defiant Jew in the face of enormous odds is the legend of David and Goliath. David's triumph over the Philistine giant was possible because of God's intervention. Modern Israel should do no less, because it has God on its side. He chides his fellow Jews for not standing bold in the face of the world:

> What is wrong with us? Who blinded us and blocked from our memories the existence and power of the G-d of Israel? Did a Jewish people exist for 2000 years without state, government, or army, wandering the earth interminably from land to land, suffering pogroms and Holocaust and surviving powerful empires that disappeared into history, just by coincidence? Did a Jewish people return to its land from the far corners of the earth to set up its own sovereign state—exactly as promised in the Bible—through mere natural means? What other nation ever did such a thing? Where are the Philistines of Goliath today? Where is imperial Rome with its Latin and its gods? Who defeats armies in six days, and on the seventh they rest?

The "deification" of Israel is finally proclaimed—Israel is a divine entity that defies the ravages of time, a militant god that defeats armies in six days and rests on the seventh!

> Who if not an Israel because there is a G-d in it! The Land of Israel is His divine Land, the State of Israel is His divine hand. History is not a series of random events, disjointed and coincidental . . . There is a Creator, a Guide, a Hand that plans and directs. There is a scenario to history. The Jew has come home for the third and last time. "But the third shall be left therein" (Zechariah 13:8).[4] "The first redemption was that from Egypt; the second, the redemption of Ezra. The third will never end" (Tanhuma, Shoftim 9).

The "restoration" of Israel to Kahane is the sanctification of the name of God *"Kiddush Hashem."* It follows that any opposition to that sanctification is defiling the name of the Lord, a most reprehensible act. Thus toleration of the Arabs' residence in Israel is *"Hillul Hashem,"* or defiling the name of the Lord:

> The State of Israel is not just one more Asian nation. It is G-d's Land, raised high—*at last!*—to put an end to the humiliation of His name. "Therefore say unto the House of Israel . . . I do this, not for your sake, O House of Israel, but rather for My holy name which you desecrated through the nations whither you came. And I will sanctify My great name that was desecrated amongst the nations . . . *and the nations shall know that I am the L-rd when I shall be sactified through you before their eyes.* And I shall take you from among the nations and gather you out of all the countries and I will bring you into your own land" (Ezekiel 36:22-24).

Thus, for at least 2000 years, according to Kahane's philosophy of history, the name of God was desecrated because Israel had not existed. Even now, the State of Israel does not conform with all the requirement necessary to restore the name of the Lord to sanctity, because it still tolerates the existence of some Arabs within its borders.

> The State of Israel is not a "political" creation. *It is a religious one.* No power could have prevented its birth and none can destroy it. It is the beginning of G-d's wrath, vengenace against the nations who ignored, disdained, and humiliated Him, who found Him irrelevant, who "knew Him not." But it is only the *beginning*. How the *final* redemption will come, and when, depends on the Jew.

Kahane exhorts the Jew to go all the way, "to sacrifice and endanger himself in order to erase the worst of all sins— the desecration of G-d's name, [*Hillul Hashem*]." This clearly means getting rid of the Arabs:

> The Arabs of Israel represent *Hillul Hashem* in its starkest form by their rejection of Jewish sovereignty over the Land of Israel despite the convenant between the L-rd of Israel and the Jews constitutes a rejection of the

> sovereignty and kingship of the L-rd G-d of Israel. Their transfer from the Land of Israel thus becomes more than a poitical issue. *It is a religious issue, a religious obligation, a commandment to erase Hillul Hashem.* Far from fearing what the Gentile will do if we do such a thing, let the Jew tremble as he considers the anger of the Almighty *if we do not*.

Kahane delivers the bottom line, "They must go," with solid conviction based on his religious faith in the G-d of Israel and fear of His wrath. This is the summation of his Zionism. But it is also the inevitable curse of Zionism in general, by definition of Zionism as the movement that asserts the distinction of the Jewish people and aims at the ingathering of the Jews into a specific land (Palestine), and at keeping Israel as a purely Jewish State. So-called secular Zionists may hesitate to declare a total expulsion of the Arabs in the Land of Israel. They have, at the least, to pay lip service to their secular-humanistic ideals. But when it comes to the Arabs in the "Land of Israel," Rabbi Meir Kahane displays no such compunctions. He is secure in his conviction that it has to be done in the name of the Torah and the G-d of Israel to bring about the redemption—a redemption which he makes a universal act of salvation. He concludes with a blood chilling call delivered with prophetic authority:

> Let us remove the Arabs from Israel and bring the redemption.

THEY MUST GO!

Goodman Smith is a freelance writer living in Chicago. He received his Ph.D. in History from the University of Chicago.

NOTES

1. A good example on the paradox of humanistic Zionist is Martin Buber, who preached tolerance towards the Arabs of Palestine, but asserted, at the same time, the distinction of the Jews and the special consecration of the "Land of Israel" (Palestine) since creation as the site of the Jewish State (see Martin Buber, *On Zion: The History of an Idea*, Schocken Books, New York, 1973, and his letter to Mahatma Gandhi, in his *Israel and the World: Essays in a Time of Crisis*, Schocken Books, New York, 1948, pp. 227-233). Buber could not explain how the Arabs would fare in such a state. At best, the great humanist was condescending in his attitude towards the "resident-strangers." At worst he was impractical if not hypocritical. Another secular zionist, Chaim Weizman, who became the first president of the State of Israel, saw the conflict between Zionist settlement in Palestine and the Arabs as " . . . a fight between a Jew and a goat," implying the destructive nature of the Arabs. (Quoted from N.A. Rose, the *Gentile Zionists: A Study in Anglo-Zionist Diplomacy, 1929-1939*. London, Frank Cass, 1973, p. 7).

2. All quotations in this article are taken from Kahane's *They Must Go*, final chapter, "Conclusion: But There is a G-d in Israel," pp. 267-276.

3. Martin Buber, *Israel and the World: Essays in a Time of Crisis*, Schocken Books, New York, 1948, p. 231.

4. Quoting this verse from Zechariah to support this argument is an example of the how-to-lie-with-scripture technique. The whole verse of Zechariah 13:8, taken from the Revised Standard Version, reads: "In the whole land, says the Lord, two thirds shall be cut off and perish, and one third shall be left alive." The same meaning is conveyed by the King James version and the Jerusalem Bible. This "prophecy" obviously refers to some kind of massacre in which two thirds of the people would perish. It cannot, by any stretch of the imagination, refer to a third and final "return."

Chapter V. The Foundations of Political Messianism in Israel

BY URIEL TAL*

The dogmatic axiom of political messianism can be summarized in the following thesis: Since Zionist work began and particularly since the Six Day War, we (Israelis) live in a transcendent political reality. Israel's military conquests during the June 1967 War reveal this metaphysical shift which can be observed in the concrete physical and political realities of everyday life. This change reached such dimensions in the holiness of "Eretz Israel" that, as Rabbi Schmaryahu Arieli concludes in his book *The Judgement of War,* the new reality is expanding and applies also in the occupied territories (including the Sinai, Sharm El-Sheikh, and the East bank of the Suez Canal).

Israel is not in the initial stage but in the midst of a Messianic era. Now Eretz Israel can liberate itself not only from political enemies, but, as Rabbi E. Hadaya states in his book *Land of Possession,* from the mystical power that incarnates the evil, the unclean and corrupted. In other words, we are entering (according to these theologians) an era when absolute holiness will imbue all souls. Through the force of war, "Shekhinah" (the divine Jewish spirit that has rested upon the Zionist enterprise from its inception) has arisen from ashes and a state of humiliation to escape its existential exile where Jews once lived. Once we have raised this divine spirit from its ashes, God forbid that we would return even one inch of that soil lest we allow the Satanic forces to prevail.

The chief spokesmen of this trend write in *Nekudah,* the official periodical of the Jewish settlement movement in the occupied areas. According to this axiom, the "War of Peace in Lebanon"was also a Holy War, a war which was a good deed. Israel's presence in Lebanon is evidence of the fulfillment of the biblical promise made in Deuteronomy 2:24: "Every place whereon the sole of your foot shall tread shall be yours: from the wilderness and Lebanon, from the river, the river Euphrates, even unto the hinder sea shall be your border".

This example is put into practice at two levels: the level of time and the level of the place in which we live. Our present time is defined by the metaphysical process of Redemption through which we are now going. Accordingly, there are two degrees of Messianic Holiness in actual time (not time as an abstract category) and this applies to the two methods used in Judaism to explain the difference between the present time and the days of the Messiah.

---

* This article by the late Uriel Tal has been translated from the Israeli daily *Ha'aretz,* 25 May 1984, and abridged by the Editors.

The first degree, according to the method of Amora Mar Shmuel (Babylonic Talmud, Tractate Berakhot 34B) in whose opinion the only difference between this world and the days of the Messiah is merely an "oppression (of Jews) by foreign kingdoms", which is an oppression of the Exile. Consequently, Messianic time finds its empirical expression in the concrete political change we have caused, which consists mainly of the abrogation of political oppression (i.e. the abrogation of the Exile). According to this method, the Messianic era is not yet an era of cosmic change. Dramatic shifts will occur in the laws of nature ("and the wolf shall dwell with the lamb, and the leopard shall crouch with the kid"). The Prophets do not mean the days of the Messiah which have already arrived but the world to come.

Rabbi Shlomo Goren, for example, in his article "The Redemption of Israel in the light of the Jewish religious law" (published in his book *"The Theory of Holidays")* quotes evidence from Maimonides. In *Halachot Teshuva* 9, 2 we find that "the days of the Messiah are this world as it is now and the world behaves according to its habits". The sole difference between them is that "the kingdom will return to Israel". Consequently, says Rabbi Goren, we may attribute a total holiness to this world not to the world to come or to an abstract mysticism, but to the concrete reality that must be fulfilled, according to the political messianic realism we are discussing. Similarly, Maimonides states in *Halachot Malachim* (Laws of Kings 12, 1) that "you must not think that in the days of the Messiah anything will change in the habits of the world, or that there will be an innovation in the acts of Genesis". Consequently, Rabbi Goren points out, there is no need to look for cosmic changes in the acts of the Creation, if you believe that the political reality of today is a Messianic reality of liberation for Jews from the oppression of Exile.

The days of the Messiah, therefore, are the days of a political change now taking place by force of Israel's weapons, and with special Heavenly support. Peace prophecies, like that of Isaiah ("and they shall beat their swords into ploughshares"), are prophecies referring to the world to come. These are not forecasts that must be implemented in this world or in the days of the Messiah.

The second degree of the Holiness of this time represents a more mystical approach and is widely believed among Gush Emunim members. It is based on the teachings of Rabbi Haya Bar Abba, who said in the name of Rabbi Yochanan (Tractate Berakhot 34:72) "All prophets have predicted the days of the Messiah only, but as for the world to come, no eye has seen, O God, except you". According to this doctrine, three conclusions are drawn:

a. All prophecies of the future which concern the drastic changes in cosmic laws are relevant now and become a practical reality both in this world and in the Messianic era.

b. All prophecies are interpreted in their simple meaning, and when it is a matter of change in the rules of the Creation, they obviously refer to the Zionist enterprise;

c. No man has the power to comprehend the life of the world to come. The present life on earth, however, is a prophetic Messianic era and not only a political Messianic era.

Here we are confronted with a poetic or more lyrical conception, such as the return to the land, life in Israel, the achievements of agriculture, and secular creativity which, as Rabbi Kook senior said, in spite of its secularity. The Zionist creativity, the military victories on the holy soil, the blood shed on this land and for this land, all these are interpreted as evidence of cosmic, and not simply political dimensions of metaphysical time. Prominent among the spokesmen and teachers of this doctrine is Rabbi Zvi Yehuda Kook. Most of the Gush Emunim's leaders grew up in the Yeshiva Merkaz Harav and were inspired by him. Rabbi Kook's doctrine teaches that the State of Israel (or the Kingdom of Israel) is the Kingdom of heaven on earth, and consequently, total Holiness embraces every Jewish person, every deed, every phenomenon, including Jewish secularism which will be swallowed one day by Holiness and Redemption.

A clear expression of the political Messianic trend appeared in a recent article titled "On the Significance of the Yom Kippur War", published in the book *Hama'alot Mimi'amakim* by Rabbi Yehuda Amital. Amital states that "one must not look at this war like we were looking at the mishaps in the days of Exile. We have to see the greatness of the hour in its Biblical dimension, and this can be seen only through a Messianic spectrum...only in the light of the Messiah". The war broke out against the background of the erection of the kingdom of Israel, which, in its metaphysical (not only symbolic) sense, is evidence of the decadence and unclean spirit in the western world. Therefore, Amital says the focus point of the Yom Kippur War is "The Gentiles fight for their very existence as Gentiles, as unclean people. The wicked fight for their survival, knowing that in the Wars of God there will be neither any room for the Devil nor for the spirit of uncleanness, nor for the remnants of western culture whose emissaries the secular Jewish people are supposed to be".

The modern, secular world, according to this conception, is fighting for its very existence. Therefore, we Jews have to fight against the uncleanness of western culture and against rationalism as such. Hence it follows that foreign culture must be annihilated, because everything foreign leads us into alien spheres and causes alienation. Such is the situation of a Jewish person who still sticks to the culture of the west and seeks a combination between Judaism and rationalistic civilization of Judaism and empirical democratic civilization. The Yom Kippur War, according to Amital's conception, must be understood in its Messianic dimension: a struggle against the whole Western civilization.

Finally, the author of "Hama'lot Mima'amakim", the basic essay of the movement under discussion, raises questions concerning why the Wars are occurring since the Messiah has come and the Kingdom of Israel has been founded. Rabbi Amital's answer to this question is that there can be one reason only: "The War begins the process of purification, the refinement and sublimation of the Jewish people". We are taught that the wars have but one meaning: God has presented us with a great mercy when He gave us the opportunity of wars. Wars purify the soul and more the uncleanness is purified through the force of war, the cleaner will the soul of Israel be. We have already conquered the lands, now we have but to conquer the uncleanness.

A second level where the axiom of the political Messianic trends finds its expression (which is principly a metaphysical conception of the political reality) is the level of the place where we live. Here, too, when we analyze the approach of the spokesmen of this trend, we refer to the original sources, because this is a group for whom the Logos is a concrete political reality. They do not quote a passage to justify an ideology, but on the contrary, the concrete reality is designed by virtue of the Logos. Indeed, historical experience has taught us, also in the twentieth century, how great the power of the Logos can be, not only to justify interests, but on the contrary: political, military and economical interests have arisen from the force of the Logos and from its ideology.

The dimension of place, therefore, parallels with time and exists primarily in a total Holiness which applies to every inch of soil and grain of dust on which our foot stands. This Holiness does not take the place of worldliness, but on the contrary, worldliness itself becomes gradually more refined and becomes a total sanctity until there is no escape for man, and every place where a Jew in the Holyland sets his foot is a sacred place. The historical symbols become objects, a materiality. The physical place, the trees and the stones, the tombs and the walls, and all other kinds of sites are sacred as such. Thus the idea of sanctity, when applied to a place, gets a meaning that is contrary to the meaning sought by symbolism, because symbolism separates the object and the significance attributed to it. The very sanctity that should be symbolized by worldly places must be referred to the places themselves.

Thus the idea of the Holiness of the land receives in this system an entirely different meaning from its meaning in Jewish tradition of the past. The main reason for the Holiness of the land was a simple matter of religious rule (according to the Mishna in Tractate Kelim, 1, 6,), "Eretz Israel is holier than all countries, and what is its Holiness? That the sheaf of corn and the First Fruit are brought from there..." That is to say, the Holiness of the land means for the Jews the possibility of fulfilling the good deeds that depend on the land. But in the sources we are discussing, the physical place becomes sacred at the expense of its historical significance, and the Holiness is not attributed to the fulfillment of the Jewish religious law, in this case an agricultural rule, of giving one tenth of the tithe to the poor, of letting him gather the corn on the edge of the field, of other good deeds depending on the land, as it was in the beginning.

The main source of this approach is the command of God given in the book called the "Objections Of Nahmaides" to the enumeration of the obligatory good deeds as fixed by Maimonides. Nahmanides says "we have been commanded to inherit the land that God has given to our forefathers, to Abraham, Isaac and Jacob, and we shall not leave it in the hands of other nations or let it become a wilderness. He told them (Numbers 33, 43) "And ye shall drive out the inhabitants of the land and swell therein, for unto you have I given the land to possess it". This command, Nahmanides continues, has been pointed out to us in the details of its borders and straits, as it is stated in Deuteronomy 1,7: "Go to the hill country of the Amorites and unto all the places high thereunto, in the Arabah, in the hill country and in the lowland, and in the South, and by the sea shore, the land of the Canaonites, and Lebanon, as far as the great river, the river Euphrates". And this has to be done says Nahmanides so that "no place of it is abandoned". The place is totally sacred.

This starting point calls now for an express policy: Relying on these sources, the Chief Rabbinate of the State of Israel has issued religious rules on the sanctity of Israeli held areas implying the political sovereignty over them and its borders proclaiming the fulfillment of a religious duty. The decision of the Chief Mount of Moriya, the place of the Temple and of the Holy of Holies, the place where the God of Israel has chosen to reside, that has been sanctified ten times by David, King of Israel. The right of the people of Israel to the Temple Mount and the site of the Holy Temple is an eternal divine right, which is irrevocable and no concessions are possible. In view of this sanctity there is no room for any compromise, neither from the viewpoint of time (temporary concessions as least, for a year or for a generation), nor concessions as far as the place is concerned.

Another decision concerns the prohibition of delivering any areas of Eretz Israel to Gentiles, including those areas we have given up in return for peace with Egypt: "According to our Holy Bible and the clear sense of the Jewish religious law, it is strictly forbidden to transfer to Gentiles the ownership of any areas in Eretz Israel", because it is santified by the "Covenant of the Pieces of the Animals". The reference to the "Covenant of the Pieces" shows us how an archaic symbol, initially a symbol of the slaughter of beasts as evidence of an alliance between ancient tribes, is a source of authority for today's policy. The return of the area's states, according to the Chief Rabbinate, is a violation of the rule of "thou shalt make no Covenant with them" (Deuteronomy 7,2). Gentiles shall not be allowed to stay in the land of Eretz Israel "and no argument of Jewish life-saving has the power to revoke this strict prohibition".

If time and place are two total existential categories, there is obviously no room here for strangers. As we have seen, these are not a bunch of crazy prophets who have gone out of their minds, or an extremist marginal minority group, but we are faced with a dogmatic system and a theology that leads necessarily to a policy that cannot tolerate the idea of human and civil rights, because this total conception of the dimension of time and place leaves no room for tolerance. This is a movement with an enormous internal power of mystical faith, and after analyzing its ideological foundations, we are facing a structure that is known to us from the political Messianism of the twentieth century. There is no room yet to compare the contents, but as far as the conceptual structure is concerned, unlike its contents, you cannot overlook here a parallel with totalitarian movements in this century.

The conclusion that follows from the theoretical structure we have mentioned (the two dimensions of time and place) appears in the form of three approaches towards the issue of human and civil rights of the non-Jew, representing three possible degrees of its solution: the restriction of rights, the denial of rights, and the most extremist level preaching genocide based on the Bible. Each of these attitudes finds expression in the sources we are discussing.

The first degree is still relatively moderate. It states that the equality of human and civil rights is a foreign democratic principle. It is essentially a European concept that alienates Jews existentially from the Holy Land. Therefore, the principle of equal rights does not apply, is not binding in our relationship with Arab residents of this country, and leaves only the status of aliens for them. Of the two types of status, the resident alien and the convert, the first is the definition of them. This is a definition used for a non-Jew who has only renounced idolatry and fulfills the seven commandments of the "Sons of Noah". A resident alien has partial rights according to the Bible, the duty of eating Kosher food does not apply to him, though he is forbidden to eat blood (Exodus 17, 13, 25, 35). He is also allowed, according to Maimonides in his Tractate of Sabbath, to work for himself on a Sabbath in public, but if he becomes employed by a Jew, he must not work for him on Sabbath.

The second attitude leads to a denial of human rights because our existence in Eretz Israel is made conditional on the emigration of the Arabs from the country. This matter was discussed in public in the issues of "Nekuda", and the institutions of the movement have already stated that the Bible has spoken in the language of men, and "one must not say a thing to which nobody listens" (i.e. at this moment the issue shocks the public so much that one should not talk for the time being about the deportation of the Arabs as an immediate action. However, the conception in principle is, that there is no room for the Arabs in the country). Therefore, the usual difference drawn in enlightened states between a civilian and a combatant is forbidden, because both the civilian and the combatant belong to the category of a population for whom there is *a prior* no room. Both are considered enemies of Israel.

The command to conquer the Land is "above the moral human considerations about the national rights of the Gentiles to our country", as Rabbi Shelomo Aviner writes in an article titled "Messianic Realism" (*Morasha,* Vol. 9). Indeed, Israel has been instructed in the Bible to "be holy", but not to be moral, and the general principles of morality, which are customary for all humanity, do not bind the people of Israel because they have been chosen to be above them.

The third attitude on the issue of a non-Jewish person's human rights is based on the Biblical command to annihilate the memory of Amalek, i.e. real genocide. This solution has found expression in an article by Rabbi Israel Hess titled: "The Command of Genocide in the Bible" (published in *"Bat Kol",* the students' organ of Bar Ilan University, on Feb. 26, 1980). The silence of most sages of Jewish Religious Law is of special significance here, because this is a group whose political leadership provides not only guidance but also absolutions. According to their conception, the Chief Rabbinate and head of yeshivot have the duty to react to reality and to react upon errors and correct them (the Rabbis in the Yoshivot are also called "supervisors"). Rabbi Hess declares: "The day will still come when we all shall be called to wage this war for the annihilation of Amalek," which is the religious commandment of genocide. The means by which the command should be carried out is specified in I Samuel 15:3: "Now go and smite Amalek, and utterly destroy all that they have and spare them not: but slay both man and woman, infant and suckling, ox or sheep, camel and ass".

This duty to annihilate Amalek has two purposes, according to Rabbi Hess: One is of racial purity, the second is an argument of warfare. The racial argument is the following: according to Genesis 36:12, Amalek is the son of Timna who was the mistress of Elipaz. But according to Deuteronomy 1:36, the same Timna was the daughter of Elipaz, and therefore Amalek's sister. Hence Rabbi Hess has concluded that Elipaz has slept with another man's wife, gave birth to his daughter Timna, took his daughter Timna as a mistress, slept with her, and thus Amalek was born. If this is true, the Rabbi tells us, it is obvious that unclean blood flows in the veins of Amalek and his children for all generations. As for the second argument, Amalek is an enemy who fought against Israel in an especially cruel way. Hess says Amalek is the incarnation of wickedness without a conscience, because the sons of Israel went on their way tired and exhausted. And Amalek attacked them and killed their mothers and sons. According to this interpretation, the antagonism between Israel and Amalek is an expression of the antagonism between light and darkness, between purity and uncleanness, between the people of God and the forces of evil. The antagonism continues to exist with regard to Amalek's children throughout all generations. And who are his children for generations? They are the Arab nations.

The conclusion of our discussion will summarize these issues by means of a structural analysis, following the method of social phenomenologists such as Peter Berger, Thomas Lackman, Alfred Schutz and others concerning the idea of *Lebenswelt* (i.e. the world, the daily experience that includes all its meaning for day to day existence). As we have seen, we are faced with a comprehensive world view and lifestyle, built as a unity that comprises and engulfs sanctity and secularity, religion and politics, heaven and earth, rights and duties. This unity creates what our sources call a "mystical realism". As a unity with a dual structure: sanctity and mysticism are referred to empirical reality, including the political realm. Rationalism and pragmatism are swallowed by the sacred realm. They do not disappear, but merge with mysticism and even shape it just as they are shaped by it.

The characteristics of this dual structure are: we live in an era of miracles, but of miracles which are empirical facts. They are at the same time part of the system of nature, of technology, and of pragmatism. Nationalism is so cosmic that it swallows and contains individualism. The individual organism has a great yearning for wide spaces, for being inside the hidden secrets of the universe until every grain of soil, every speck of dust and ashes become part of the universe and its spaces. Furthermore, the conquest of land is also a conquest of earthliness and its purification. It purifies the country from everything alien, from every uncleanness. It is purification that is so comprehensive and total until it absorbs also the personal self-purification of the individual, and redeems it from alienation. The political ecstasy, paradoxically, is a means by which the settler not only cultivates his country but also his mind, and the whole reality in which we live is a reality of liberation from existential alienation within the Zionist enterprise, that is carried out in practice, in the concrete political realm.

Thus we may conclude, that we are faced with a political Messianism, where the individual, the people, and the land achieve an organic unification under the wings of an absolute sanctity. It is based upon a metaphysical conception of the political realm that finds its expression in a total conception of time and place. The danger of this totality lies in the fact that it leads to a totalitarian concept of the political realm because within its framework there is no room for the existence of the human and civil rights of a non-Jew.

Chapter VI. The Third Temple and a red heifer

BY ISRAEL SHAHAK*

The trial of the Jewish underground terror organization has revealed the existence of forces in Judaism whose serious purpose is not only "the purification of Temple Mount from the hold of Islam on it" (as confessed by defendant No. 2 and quoted in *Ha'aretz* on 4 June 1984) but the rebuilding of the Third Temple and the restoration of sacrifices in it. It is interesting to note in this context that not one orthodox rabbi in Israel has said a word against those two aims. Therefore, it is important to investigate why, despite the great and central role which the sacrificial system and the Temple play in the living Jewish religion and tradition, no attempt was made, until recently, to realize this deeply felt wish. How can the fact that the great majority of orthodox rabbis prohibit Jews to ascend Temple Mount be reconciled with the wish to rebuild the Third Temple?

The answers can be found readily enough, and some of them are now freely discussed in Hebrew. Unfortunately, most of the information required in order to understand this problem, or for that matter most problems of Judaism as it really is, are simple not available in English. I will try to indicate briefly what the problem in Jewish religious terms actually is, and how the Jewish fanatics attempt to solve it.

Until about the sixth century AD, the practice of Judaism included an intricate system of laws of purity and impurity of the body (and also of vessels used for eating or drinking). According to those laws there are several sources of impurity, the chief and most dangerous being the dead body of a Jew, which is regarded as both sacred and impure. Any Jew who comes into even the most indirect contact with a Jewish corpse or its remains becomes impure: a walk in a cemetery or being present in a hospital or house which may contain a corpse is sufficient. Once a Jew is impure, he remains so forever, unless he is purified in a special manner described in the Old Testament (Numbers 19), and much elaborated in the Talmud. Briefly, apart from washing and engaging in other ceremonies, a red heifer must be sacrificed and burned to ashes. Part of the ashes, mixed with water and applied in a special manner, have the unique property of purifying an impure Jew who is otherwise prohibited, on pain of horrible penalties, from carrying out certain religious duties. Offering sacrifices in the temple and even entering it are two of the religious acts for which purity is absolutely required; these rules were stricly obeyed in ancient times. The red heifer was sacrificed from time to time, actually on the Mount of Olives, not in the temple itself, and its ashes were used to purify the priest and certain people who would enter Temple Mount, or take part in other sacred occasions. However, the last ashes were lost around the sixth century AD, and from then on all Jews are held to be impure.

The sanctity of Temple Mount remains, however, and this is why pious Jews

---

(Reprinted with permission from Middle East International, 22 March 1984)

regard it as a sin of desecration to enter it. According to the Jewish religious law all non-Jews are impure and have no means of purifying themselves, not even through the ashes of a red heifer. Hence their presence on Temple Mount is an even greater desecration. In fact, many appeals have been made to the Israeli government by "moderate" fanatics to forcefully close Temple Mount altogether and so prevent everybody from entering it.

Another example, which illustrates how this problem can have immediate practical implications, concerns the airplanes overflying Temple Mount. According to the more modern rabbinical interpretations, the sanctity of Temple Mount, violated by impure persons, extends infinitely upwards. One of the attractions offered by El Al's South African flights used to be that it planes would, when returning from South Africa, pass over the Red Sea and Eilat and then overfly Jerusalem and Temple Mount at a rather low altitude. The passengers could thereby admire the view, but by being impure they also committed the sin of desecration. I am happy to record the following campaign by many rabbis and all the religious parties, at least this sin is no longer being committed. El Al was given, about a year ago, strict orders not to allow its planes to enter the sacred air space above Temple Mount.

Now, why don't Jewish fanatics just sacrifice another red heifer, purify themselves and enter Temple Mount free of sin? Here, we find ourselves in the perfect "Catch 22" situation: only pure Jewish priests can make the sacrifice, but without the ashes of a red heifer they remain impure. No practical solution has yet been found to this problem, although several of either a hilarious or hopeful nature have been proposed. Thus, a learned journal proposed in the late 60s to find a pregnant woman from a priestly family and isolate her shortly before the birth of her child in a separate room inside a house built on thin pillars (to minimize the contact with any Jewish corpse that might be buried underneath the house). She would then be delivered by robots, and the infant, assuming it was a boy, would be raised, as in a science-fiction story, by robots, until he reached adulthood at the age of 13. He could then become a pure Jewish priest, sacrifice the red heifer and all could be well. More practical-minded fanatics propose a dig under Temple Mount, since sanctity according to the rabbis extends upwards, not downwards, in order to find the ashes of the red heifer in a buried jar. In my opinion, some rabbis are quite capable of declaring that some old-looking jar really contains such ashes, just as some of those now accused of membership of the Jewish terror group seriously declared a few years ago that the roof beams of the al-Aqsa mosque had come from the Second Temple, destroyed in 70 AD.

Barring such solutions, there are only two ways out. One, adopted by the older rabbis, holds that one must wait for the Messiah, who, together with his traditional attendant Elias the Prophet will solve all problems. The other, which has strong roots in Jewish mysticism, holds that for the sake of the greater good and since we are coming to the End of Days, the very pious may commit "necessary" sins of all kinds which then cease to be sins and become good deeds. I am afraid that many Jewish fanatics are quite advanced in this direction.

Chapter VII. Apartheid Theology: A Critique

BY AN ANONYMOUS AFRICAN THEOLOGIAN

The Biblical story of Israel can be read in one of two different ways: Either as the story of a small and oppressed people who struggled against the most overwhelming odds and survived as a dignified, self-conscious people, or as the story of an arrogant and intolerant people who believed that they were chosen of God to dominate the earth. Clearly a critical reading of the Bible will show both these readings to be biased. Yet theologians as well as politicians and other would-be formers of public opinion are well known for a non-critical use of Scripture and the tendency to seize on Biblical images to bolster an already formed opinion or ideology.

I. The use of the concept "Israel" in western theology.

The concept of "Israel" is used in different ways and to different ends in different kinds of western thought. I illustrate one particularly common usage of the concept in what might be broadly described as liberation-type western theologies. Mention is made in passing of three such theologies.

1.1 American civil religion.

American civil religion first emerged with the arrival of White settlers in the so called New World. They came to be regarded as the founding fathers of the United States, in spite of the generations of native people who lived there before them. They engendered within themselves a sense of special destiny among peoples of the earth and were inwardly motivated by themes of a "promised land", a "new Israel" and a people "destined to be a light among nations." From then on the stage was set for White Americans to invade not only American-Indian territory and to virtually destroy their culture and heritage, but ultimately to shape and manipulate areas well beyond the geographical limits of that the Western world — in South East Asia, South America and the Middle East.

The story of this American rise to power is an interesting and curious one. The story of Israel, a people who were once slaves in Egypt and despised by their oppressors, fired the hearts of the poor and disinherited of Britain and Europe as they fled religious, social and political persecution and oppression in *their own* exodus from the Old World to the New. This is the saga of a people who once saw themselves to be political "strangers to the convenants of promise (and) having no hope" who were now — again politically — "no longer strangers and sojouners, but . . . fellow citizens with the saints and members of the household of God" (Ephesians 2: 13.20). Driven by this self-understanding American *capitalism* would flourish (c.f. Max Weber's *The Protestant Ethic), cultural domination* would expand

and *military strength* develop to frightening proportions.

The concepts of a "new Israel", "the exodus" and "the promised land" in American civil religion which had uplifted the homeless exiles of Europe in their American dream ultimately turned into an aggressive determination to rule the world.

1.2 Apartheid-theology

Early White Afrikaner settler theology also adopted the Biblical images of Israel as the basis of its self-understanding — as frontier farmers and later the trekkers into the hinterland were engaged in conflict with the Black inhabitants of the land and the might of the British Empire. The Voortrekker leader M.W. Pretorius addressed his aged countrymen as "fathers of Israel" and compared them to "the Lord's chosen" who had fled from the English in the Cape as the Israelites escaped from Pharoah in Egypt. Their encounter with Blacks revealed a similar self-understanding. They looked upon these inhabitants as unbelieving Canaanites and regarded themselves as entering into the promised land as did Israel before them. They understood themselves to be "instruments of God's hand to put an end to plunder, murder and violence among them (the heathen!) . . . and promote the extension of Christian civilization among thousands whose existence hitherto had been rooted in darkness".

A decisive point in Afrikaner history came when some 470 trekkers, having sworn a vow to God, defeated a mighty Zulu army of approximately 10,000 men. In spite of attempts by some intellectuals to attribute this victory to superior weapons or the like, popular Afrikaner belief still has it that God intervened that day on behalf of His chosen people in Africa. This deep belief in a God-given mission, sustained by Biblical texts which referred to Israel of old, has sustained the Afrikaner in some of the darkest moments of his history — and when finally he attained independence from Britain and the Republic was about to dawn, Dr. H.F. Verwoerd, the architect of apartheid, could only conclude, "perhaps it was intended that we should have been planted here — that from this might emanate the story whereby all that has been built up since the days of Christ may be maintained for the good of all mankind."

This type of Afrikaner civil religion which became the basis of White domination and apartheid theology also has, like American civil religion, its intriguing historical contours. One can only be moved by the early struggle of the Afrikaner against chauvinistic British imperialism and economic exploitation. But then the ironic twist came and through uncompromising legislation he was to deprive Blacks of the country of the very freedom he had attained for himself. Individual Afrikaners have repeatedly reminded their fellow Afrikaners of the similarities between the present Black liberation struggle and that of their own at the turn of the century — but to no avail. What was once a liberation theology has become an ideology of oppression.

1.3 Black theology

Black Theology, particularly of the American brand, through exponents like James Cone, Albert Cleage, Washington and others have also used the Biblical symbols of Israel in their theological exercises. In one way or another each of these theologians regard Blacks to stand in a special chosen relationship to God. The suffering of Blacks is for a specific purpose; in order that they may be released from bondage, experience social as well as personal salvation and attain both political and economic liberation. We read of Blacks being the "suffering servant" of God, of the "black exodus", the "black messiah", the "black madonna", the "promised land" and the "black nation of Israel". It is also interesting to note that Black Theologians tend to employ the same basic Biblical texts to support their arguments as do Afrikaner theologians and American civil religionists.

Without suggesting that Black Theology is identical to the other types of theology identified above, the similarities are sufficient for both Black and White proponents of Liberation Theology to warn against falling into the trap which changed American and Afrikaner religions into something less than liberation.

II. The enduring influence of the "Israel" mentality in contemporary political thought.

In more recent times, both American civil religion and Afrikaner self-understanding have more or less divested themselves of the explicit use of such Biblical themes as identified above. Yet that the basic "Israel" mentality has endured can probably be discerned from the amount of mutual assistance and support that exists between the United States and Israel on the one hand, and South Africa and Israel on the other. The nature of this mutual co-operation is too well known to spell-out in any detail. Recently, the Prime Minister at the time, Mr. John Vorster, paid an extended visit to Israel; world news journals speculate on the extent of military collaboration between South Africa and Israel; trade agreements are entered into and cultural exchange programmes encouraged. The one anti-Jewish stance of early Afrikanerdom — when the capitalist exploiter of Afrikaner workers was scornfully depicted in cartoons as a large and sumptuous Jewish business magnate, called Mr. Hoggenheimer, consuming the poor workers of the day — has virtually disappeared. Talk of a Jewish backed world conspiracy to dominate the world through financial institutions still raises its head from time to time, but this certainly does not enjoy government support. Pro-nazi, anti-Jewish student pranks continue to be seen but these are severely censured, and the pro-Hitler stance of some Afrikaners in the thirties is securely tucked away out of sight or sound.

These are the embarrassments of the past. Today Israel is held up as an example to be followed. Her will to resist the Arab world is admired, her military skill praised, Jewish independence exalted and Zionist fervour affirmed as a legitimate form of nationalism and pride. These all have their counterparts in White South Africa's resistance — a determination to resist Black Africa, the need for White independence, Whitist identity and pride, and the military muscle to ensure all this is maintained for as long as possible. Sermons are still preached and political speeches are still made, which with subtle innuendo remind South Africans that like Israel of Old they need to stand firm against the forces of change and world upheaval. In a word, White South Africa is sustained in her will to resist by the Elijah complex which says "I only am left and they seek my life, to take it away." Any truth that some may find in this attitude is soon lost in the ideological use made of it to resist fundamental change on the part of Whites. Whites are thus able to persuade themselves that their recalcitrance is ultimately of God, and that any legitimate claims by Blacks are the modern equivalent of Baal worship — namely communism.

(The above article was reprinted with permission of the Presbyterian Church U.S.A. Its author, an African theologian, wishes to remain anonymous).

Chapter VIII. Implications of the Israel-South Africa Alliance

BY MARWAN BUHEIRY

The intimate connection between Zionism, Israel, South Africa and Imperialism is indeed a long one; in broad terms it has gone through three phases. Beginning with the late 1890's it involved Theodor Herzl, Cecil Rhodes, and Joseph Chamberlain, Britain's Colonial Secretary, and the quest for vast colonization schemes of Jewish settlement in the Arab World and Africa. The second phase (1917 to 1950) dominated by such figures as Chaim Weizmann, General Ian Smuts, Lord Balfour, and Lloyd George was principally concerned with extracting a British promise for a Jewish national home in Palestine, consolidating Zionist presence during the Mandate period, and paving the way for recognition of a Zionist state. Following the establishment of Israel in 1948 the connection entered a third phase, characterized by increased interdependence in the military, economic, geopolitical, psychological and particularly in the nuclear and advanced technological fields.

Whereas the first two phases of the connection involved a triangular relationship combining the interests of the World Zionist Organization (WZO), South Africa, and Imperial Britain, the third phase has taken the direction of a bilateral symbiosis between South Africa and Israel. Neverthcless, the third component of the triangle has not altogether disappeared; in fact, it has been diversified and strenthened by additions from the European community nations and the United States which aims, ever since Vietnam, at "the formation of special relationships with regional subimperial powers so that military intervention could be delegated to junior partners."(*)

It is abundantly clear that this close association of interests which today has grown into interdependence of the two colonial outposts (or regional subimperial powers), presents grave implications to the Arab World and more generally the Third World as the foregoing analysis will show. Soon after the UN Security Council imposed an arms embargo on South Africa in November 1977, the Israeli ambassador to Johannesburg proclaimed that it was more important than ever for Israel and South Africa to stick together in order to confront the alliance of Africa and the Arab World.(**)

(*) Richard Falk, "Exporting Counter Revolution" *The Nation,* June 9, 1979, p. 659. See also James H. Mittleman, "America's Investment in Apartheid" *The Nation,* June 9, 1979, pp. 684-689.

(**) Two Syrian scholars have contributed perceptive critiques of the Israel-South Africa experience: George Jabbour, *Settler Colonialism in Southern Africa and the Middle East* (Beirut: Palestine Liberation Organization Research Center, 1970) and George J. Tohmeh, *the Unholy Alliance: Israel and South Africa* (New York: New World Press, 1973).

Theodor Herzl, Cecil Rhodes and Joseph Chamberlain: Phase One

Large scale colonization projects in progress in South Africa during the last decade of the nineteenth century involving mechanized mining, advanced technology, and substantial investments fascinated Theodor Herzl. From the evidence of his principal treatise *The Jewish State* written in 1895 and of his utopian novel *Altneuland,* it is clear that the South African experience served as inspiration, model, and source of funds; the South African wing of the Zionist movement being, in relative terms, one of the wealthiest.

Following his official appointment as head of the Zionist movement at the Basle Congress of 1897, Herzl sought to link Zionism to the rising fortunes of Great Britain using the argument of Jewish colonization at strategic locations in the Near East and Africa in close support of Britain's imperial aims. England was to him the "Archimedean point" for the Zionist enterprise and in this respect he suggested to Lord Rothschild the sponsorship of an extensive colonization blueprint in Sinai, Palestine, and Cyprus: "You may claim high credit from your goverment," he wrote in 1902 to the acknowledged leader of Britain's Jews, "if you strengthen British influence in the Near East by a substantial colonization of our people at the strategic point where Egyptian and Indo-Persian interests converge."[1]

In much the same vein Herzl also unfolded to the British Colonial Secretary, Joseph Chamberlain, a comprehensive Zionist colonization project backed by "a Jewish Eastern Company with 5 pound sterling capital" for settlements in Cyprus and the Sinai (Al-Arish).[2] It is interesting to note in passing that one of the Zionist movement's foremost colonial experts was a South African Jewish engineer, Leopold Kessler, who was sent on a mission to the Sinai in 1903 to assess the Al-Arish project. Joseph Chamberlain was somewhat hesitant about Cyprus, more enthusiastic about Al-Arish, and finally offered his own "Uganda project" to Herzl, involving a Jewish colonial settlement in a prime agricultural region of the East African — actually Kenyan — colonial domain. The motivation for the offer was largely a consequence of events in South Africa. In the aftermath of a ruinous Boer War, which ended with the victory of the British over the Boers of South Africa, particularly in such sectors as mining, industry, real estate, and general postwar reconstruction. The Rand Territory in South Africa, famed for its fabulous wealth, was even then largely under control of Jewish promoters and investors who were also some of the principal figures of the rising South Africa Zionist movement. The Colonial Secretary felt that the Ugandan project would further consolidate Jewish presence in the African continent within, of course, a British imperialist framework; it is therefore not surprising that South African Zionists enthuiastically endorsed what Israel Zangwill called a "British-Jewish Crown Colony" in reference to the Ugandan project.[3]

Yet another noteworthy example of the "Triangular" relationship is Theodor Herzl's admiration of Cecil Rhodes, the archetypal model of the successful colonizer whom he sought to emulate especially in connection with the British South African Company. Despite strenuous efforts, a meeting with Rhodes could not be arranged but Herzl's *Diaries* contain the text of a revealing memorandum addressed to Rhodes on January 11, 1902 which was not actually sent: "How do I happen to turn to you seeing this is a matter so remote to you? How? Because it is colonial, and because it presupposes an understanding of a development that requires twenty to thirty years."[4] To the founding father of the movement, Zionism was indeed a colonial movement requiring the sponsorship of British imperialism. And as Dr. Jabbour has shown in his study *Settler-Colonialism in Southern Africa and the Middle East,* from the very beginning the Zionist project was perceived and executed in terms of settler-colonalism.

Weizmann and Smuts: Phase Two

The long personal friendship between General Ian Christian Smuts, principal architect of the South African state, and Chaim Weizmann, a leading Zionist figure and Israel's first president, was an important contributing factor in the gains achieved by the Zionist movement since the outbreak of the First World War. But this relationship is also significant in other aspects. For, as Richard Stevens in his study *Weizmann and Smuts: A Study in Zionist-South African Cooperation,* has cogently argued: "It helps to put in perspective the contradictions of western liberalism and the psychological climate which rationalized the dominant position of a white minority in South Africa and of a new European settlement in Palestine. It also underscores the crucial relationship between Zionism and South Africa, a relationship drawing its strength first from the Zionist character of the South African Jewish community with its privileged economic position, secondly, from the very nature of the South African economic-political system and thirdly, from the imperial factor as it affected South Africa's domestic and international situation."[5]

It is remarkable that the same handful of leading politicians decided the political future of both South Africa and Palestine: Lord Milner, Lord Selbourne, Lord Balfour, Joseph Chamberlain, and General Smuts contributed to the birth of the South African Union of *1910* and to the Balfour Declaration of *1917.* In both cases the idea was to place power in the hands of those who, to use the words of Balfour. "think like us"[6]. An African majority was thus placed under a minority of white masters and an Arab majority was left to the tender mercies of an East European minority of settler-colonists — the Zionist Organization — in Palestine. The rationale, a legitimizing of inequality, as spelled out by Balfour, was: "You cannot give the natives in South Africa equal rights with the whites without threatening the whole fabric of white civilization."[7] Or as Lord Curzon remarked to Balfour shortly after the publication of the Balfour Declaration in reference to the real aims of the Zionist Executive in Palestine: "He that is Weizmann contemplates a Jewish state, a Jewish nation, a subordinate population of Arabs ruled by Jews; the Jews in possession of the fact of the land and directing the administration."[8]

To be sure, General Smuts realized that Zionism was part and parcel of the imperial scheme, particularly in that crucial strategic area, the Palestine-Suez Canal axis, at the very crossroads of Africa and Asia. Furthermore he appreciated, as Chamberlain had done, the vital economic role of Jews in South Africa and their strong commitment to Zionism and to the imperial ideal. Similarly Chaim Weizmann, who had become a British subject in 1910, believed that the success of his movement depended on the link with British imperialism and, in return, viewed a Zionist Palestine as "a very great asset to the British Empire."[9] In this respect he adhered closely to Herzl's political vision. Writing to Balfour from Palestine in 1918, he drew attention to the intimate nature of this relationship: "I see that the welfare of Zionism is intimately linked up with the strength of British policy in the East, and I feel that London, Cairo, Jerusalem and Delhi, are very intimately connected, and the weakness of a link in this important chain may have serious consequences."[10]

The outbreak of World War One and the fateful participation of the Ottoman Empire on the German side provided Weizmann with the opportunity to lead somewhat disclosed Zionist Movement along Herzlian paths. In 1914 he suggested to a friend: "We can reasonably say that should Palestine fall within the British sphere of influence and should Britain encourage a Jewish settlement there, as a British dependency, we could have in twenty to thirty years a million Jews out there, perhaps more: They would develop the country, bring back civilization to it and form a very effective guard for the Suez Canal."[11] The simplistic arrogance of the civilization mission which rationalized all European expansion, is also revealed elsewhere in his writings. In a paper entitled "The Position in Palestine" (1929) he viewed the Zionist enteprise as the fight between "progress and stagnation", between "civilization and the desert."[12]

Chaim Weizmann contributed to the wartime effort by placing his scientific skill at the disposal of the Ministry of Munitions; his discoveries in the production of acetone for high explosives were recognized as valuable. He was therefore well placed to build upon the contacts of his predecessor Herzl with the British ruling circles. Lord Balfour, Winston Churchill, Lord Selbourne, Lord Milner, General Smuts and Lloyd George became the target of his interested friendship. And these, to be sure, played a prominent role in the formulation of the Balfour Declaration and the implementation of postwar imperial policy in the Near East.

Having secured a major political gain in the form of a Declaration, which, for all its ambiguity, recognized Zionist aspirations, Weizmann's next task was to extract the maximum advantage from its promises. This clearly meant, in practice, that the rights of the Palestinian Arabs would be trampled upon without any hesitation.

The first years of Zionist consolidation in Palestine with the active help of an imposed Mandate system coincided with the period of General Smut's first ministry, 1919-1924. In South Africa the General pursued anti-African policies which culminated in the Port Elizabeth and Bulhock (1921) massacres and the Native Affairs Act excluding Africans from Parliamentary life. At the same time he sought the help of the powerful South African Jewish community while extending considerable support to the World Zionist Organization. Speaking in Johannesburg in November 1919, Smuts spelt out his view of the common bond between Boer culture in South Africa and Jewish tradition as he interpreted it. "I need not remind you" he said in his address to the South African Jewish Board of Deputies and the Zionist Federation, "that the white people of South Africa, and especially the older Dutch population, have been brought up almost entirely on Jewish traditions." And he added: "We are standing together on a common platform, the greatest spiritual platform the world has ever seen. On that platform I want us to build the future of South Africa."[13]

Thus for more than three decades (1917-1950), whether in office or out, General Smuts supported the Zionist cause, using his considerable influence in the British corridors of power to further its fortune; and Weizmann could always count on a swift and effective reponse to urgent calls for help. This included, first and foremost, the Balfour Declaration and was followed in 1920 by a joint Weizmann-Smuts attempt to extend the northern and eastern borders of the Palestine mandate in order to expand the potential for Jewish colonization to the Litani River in South Lebanon and beyond the River Jordan.[14] The South African Prime Minister actively defended the Zionist policy of large scale immigration which was being accomplished in total disregard of Arab views and apprehensions and of the country's absorption capacity; and he also sponsored fund-raising campaigns in South Africa with frequent personal appearances on platforms.

Smuts political support was especially crucial in the wake of such revolutionary Palestinian reactions to the growing threat of the Zionist presence as the Jaffa Rebellion in 1921, the concerted actions on Zionist colonial settlements in 1929, and notably during the Palestinian National Revolt of 1936. Smuts frequent high level interventions to undermine the Palestinian Arab case and his successful attempts to thwart the initiation and implementation of an evenhanded Mandate policy were decisive in preserving Zionist gains, particularly in the sphere of immigration and land acquisitions. Smuts worked closely with Weizmann to present Arab nationalism as a *threat* to Britain's imperial geopolitical position, and Zionism as a valuable prop.

During the Second World War and its immediate aftermath, a period with fateful consequences to Palestine, the South African leader assisted Zionist diplomacy to counter the meagre Arab influence in America, particularly during the San Francisco conference, and to oppose some of the recommendations of the Anglo-American Committee of Inquiry on Palestine. He also placed the resources of the South African delegation to the United Nations at its disposal. Finally, he completed the work started with the Balfour Declaration by extending *de facto* recognition to the state of Israel on May 24, 1948; *de jure* recognition following two days later.

One of the most interesting manifestations of the triangular connection, Zionism-Britain-South Africa, is Weizmann's "Memorandum on Africa" addressed to Smuts in 1943: a remarkable post-war plan of development for the African continent, which aimed, in effect, at reinforcing British and South African imperialism by economic means. In short he was advocating a brand of neo-colonialism aimed at safeguarding their plunder of strategic raw materials. Weizmann's scheme "based on the assumption", as he put it, "that Africa will probably become the backbone of the British Colonial Empire after this war," involved extensive utilization of carbohydrates for a new chemical industry to replace petroleum and coal.[15] And, of course, a special place in the project was reserved for the Jewish National Home: it would serve as "the laboratory or the pilot-plant for the big factory into which the African Continent under this scheme might eventually develop."[16]

One must also recall the fact that many prominent South African Jewish figures, including Abba Eban, Arthur Lourie, and Major Comay, joined the ranks of Israel's ruling elite: all three assumed prominent positions in the diplomatic infrastructure of the newly-founded Jewish state.

Post 1948 Symbiosis: Phase Three

The death of General Smuts in 1950 brought to a close one of the many chapters in the South African-Zionist Israel connection. To be sure, the cooperation — or better still, the Phase Three of symbiosis — is closer today than it ever was. Their everyday perceptions of each other as reflected in the press, their strong collaboration in the military and economic fields, their updated versons of the Weizmann "Memorandum" (Israel as a 'pilot-plant for the big factory' of South Africa), and the April 1976 visit by the South African Prime Minister Vorster, to Israel, are all eloquent reminders. The Sharpeville massacre by the South African regime is paralleled by the equally brutal routine of Israeli massacres in the West Bank and in South Lebanon. The organ of the National Party of South Africa, *Die Burgher,* had put it succinctly on May 29, 1968: "Israel and South Africa have a common lot. Both are engaged in a struggle for existence, and both are in constant clash with the decisive majorities in the United Nations . . .; it is South Africa's interest that Israel is successful in containing her enemies, who are among South Africa's own most vicious enemies."[17] It is therefore neither surprising to find the two states actively in concert against national liberation movements, nor to note the magnitude of the association in the armaments industry which is far above what is officially revealed and recognized. This is of particular importance in the combat aircraft and naval industries: the Kfir fighter, the Reshef patrol-boat, and Gabriel guided missile are the most recent vivid examples. But it also extends to other weapons systems; South Africa and Israel have supplied tanks to each other at various times and Israel regularly exports light weapons, sophisticated electronic systems, and anti-guerrilla equipment to the South African state specifically designed to fight Third World liberation movements.

In November 1977 the *Economist* (London) revealed that "Kissinger in early 1975 secretly asked the Israeli government to send troops to Angola in order to cooperate with the South African army in fighting the Popular Movement . . . Israel sent in some military instructors specializing in anti-guerrilla warfare plus equipment designed for the same purpose."[18]

Equally extensive is the scope and volume of economic cooperation: export and import of raw materials, diamonds and finished products; investment and financing; and the exchange of production techniques. This has been neatly characterized by Itzhak Unna, Israel's ambassador to the apartheid state in 1974: "With South Africa's abundance of raw materials and Israel's know-how, we can really go places if we join forces."[19] Yet another example of close communion, one with sinister overtones and implications for the not too distant future, is in the nuclear field — especially as South Africa is one of the world's principal producers of uranium. Israel, for its part, contributes its advanced nuclear technology in the field of lasers, in the chemical reprocessing of nuclear material, and in the clandestine testing of nuclear devices. Both states have refused to sign the nuclear non-proliferation treaty. "I would also like to provide two additional concrete examples of the close identity of their ideological perceptions: There are perhaps only two countries in the world where Transkei's "independence" was celebrated: South Africa and Israel. On the evening of October 28, 1976, Israeli television viewers watched a special program on the new Transkei prepared by South African television. In addition, news events in Africa are routinely described in Israeli mass media from the perspective of minority settler-colonial regimes. The Soweto incidents were portrayed in the Vorster government's version as "criminal violence created by communist elements and outside agitators."*

To conclude, in recalling the long standing connection from Herzl and Rhodes, to Weizmann and Smuts, to Rabin and Vorster, and most importantly today, one ought not to lose sight of the basic impulses which have served to reinforce their community of interests in the political, military, economic and colonial spheres. In the words of one analyst "each took for granted the moral legitimacy of the other's position. Thus, not a word is to be found in Weizmann's correspondence or writings questioning either the racial basis of the South African state on which Zionism was so dependent or Smuts' role in upholding its racist system: the subordinate position of the African majority in South Africa posed no moral difficulty (for Weizmann) ... Similarly, Smuts assumed without question 'the right' of Jewish settlers to occupy Palestine without regard to the rights of the indigenous Palestinian Arabs. In both cases, Smuts and Weizmann epitomized the capacity of western civilization to rationalize domination and exploitation, conquest and control . . ."[20] And it is abundantly clear that the increased isolation of the two states has reinforced such characteristics: to use the explosive statement of former South African Prime Minister Dr. Verwoerd whose authority on the nature and function of apartheid is clearly manifest, "the Jews took Israel from the Arabs after the Arabs had lived there a thousand years. In that I agree with them, Israel, like South Africa is an apartheid state."[21] It is interesting to note that Verwoerd was eulogized by the Chief Rabbi of South Africa as "the first man to give apartheid a moral basis."*

Throughout the three phases the implication to the Arab World of this cooperation and interdependence have been particularly grave. In the broadest terms one would begin with the general phenomenon of imperialism of the post-1880 era; a seamless web encompassing the globe with key strategic constructs such as the Route to India and the Cape to Cairo Route. Today the emphasis is also on the direct policing of the Red Sea and the Indian Ocean. In addition, there was, and there still is, the

---

Benjamin Beit-Hallahmi*, "South Africa and Israel's Strategy of Survival" *New Outlook*, April-May 1977, pp. 56-57.

Robert G. Weisbord*, "The Dilemma of South African Jewry" *Journal of Modern African Studies*, 5, 2 (1967) pp. 233-241; also Madison Area Committee on Southern Africa, *South Africa and Israel* (Wisconsin, 1971) p. 1.

economic plunder of the Third World and the enforced colonization of the land. A South African was Theodor Herzel's expert on colonization with a specific mission to examine the Zionist al-Arish project in Sinai in 1903. General Ian Smuts, the principal architect of the South African state, closely identified with Chaim Weizmann and the project to construct a Zionist state during the Mandate period. He exerted considerable influence in London to advance the cause of Zionist immigration and territorial gains and to neutralize the struggle of the Palestinian Arabs for independence and nationhood. Smuts also lent valuable support to Weizmann during the Second World War and at the San Francisco conference. In more recent times one would also recall the sponsorship by South Africans of *moshav* colonization projects such as the Neot Hakikar settlement.*

Today the interdependence has reached new heights both in conventional armaments and in the nuclear field. The implications are obvious and the challenge to the Arab and African worlds is clear.

* *Jerusalem Post,* Dec. 18, 1974, p. 3.

Notes

1. *Richard P. Stevens, Weizmann and Smuts: A Study in Zionist-South African Cooperation* (Beirut: The Institute for Palestine Studies, 1975). p. 16.
2. *Ibid.,* p. 17.
3. Israel Zangwill, *The Voice of Jerusalem* (N.Y.: Macmillan, 1921) p. 254.
4. Theodor Herzl, *The Complete Diaries,* Vol. III, pp. 1193-1194. The Memorandum of Jan., 1902 was not sent. Cecil Rhodes died shortly thereafter in March, 1902.
5. Stevens, *op. cit.,* p. ix.
6. *Ibid.,* p. xi.
7. *Ibid.*
8. Quoted in Christopher Mayhew and Michael Adams, *Publish it Not: The Middle East Cover Up* (London: Longman, 1975). pp. 1444-145.
9. Leonard Stein, *Weizmann and England* (London: W.H. Allen, 1964), p. 15.
10. *Ibid.,* pp. 15-16.
11. Weizmann, *Trial and Error,* p. 191.
12. C. Weizmann, "the Position in Palestine", *Palestine Papers,* no. 2 (Jewish Agency for Palestine, London, 1929-30), pp. 24-25.
13. Stevens, *op. cit.,* p. 33.
14. *Ibid.,* p. 34.
15. *Ibid.,* p. 124.
16. *Ibid.,* pp. 126-127.
17. "Israel-South Africa: Cooperation of Imperialistic Outposts" edited by Third World Magazine, (Bonn: P.D.W., 1976), p. 18.
18. *Economist,* November, 1977, p. 90.
19. *Financial Mail,* June 1974. Quoted in "Israel-South Africa: Cooperation of Imperialistic Outposts", p. 49.
20. Stevens, *op. cit.,* p. x.
21. Rand Daily Mail, November 23, 1961. Quoted in "Israel-South Africa Cooperation of Imperialistic Outposts", p. 12.

(Reprinted with permission from the Presbyterian Church U.S.A. Dr. Buheiry is Professor of Political Science at American University, Beirut-Lebanon).

Conclusion: Nation Against Nation

BY NICHOLAS WOLTERSTORFF

At certain points in the life of some nations a new phenomenon arises—*nationalism.* Nationalism is best understood, I think, as a nation's preoccupation with its own nationhood. Instead of its members simply living their life together as a nation, they become preoccupied with their national existence—rather like the man who constantly checks his pulse rather than simply going about his tasks and letting his heart do its work. It is possible for this self-preoccupation to be stirred up by members of the people who, in one way or another, have come to the conviction that there is something lacking in the national life. More customarily, however, nationalism is the response of a nation to its conviction that it has been wronged, that an injustice has been done it, that it has not received its due. In the words of Isaiah Berlin, it is customarily the result of "the infliction of a wound on the collective feeling of a society, or at least of its spiritual leaders."[1] In any case, whatever its origins, the function of nationalism

> is to indicate disease. Bodily organs do not draw attention to themselves until they are attacked by disease. Similarly, nationalism is at bottom the awareness of some lack, some disease or ailment. The people feels a more and more urgent compulsion to fill this lack, to cure this disease or ailment. The contradiction between the immanent task of the nation and its outer and inner condition has developed or been elaborated and this contradiction affects the feeling of the people. What we term nationalism is their spiritual reaction to it.[2]

The wound that provokes nationalism comes in many different varieties. The context of our discussion makes it especially important to notice that colonialism has proved to be one of those wounds: in seeing this, we begin to see some of the connections between nation and economy in our modern

*Reprinted with permission of the author and Eerdmunns Publishing Co., Grand Rapids, Michigan.

world-system. The surge of nationalism after the Second World War was the response of the nations of the Third World to the exploitation and oppression and humiliation that they suffered at the hands of their colonial masters.

It will be evident that economic exploitation and political oppression can be the wounds that provoke nationalism. Let me emphasize that humiliation and paternalism—being treated without respect—can also be the wound. And we know enough about colonialism to say that the colonial masters invariably regarded their colonial subjects as inferior human beings, if indeed they noticed them at all—for typical of colonialism is a curious ambivalence between regarding the conquered land as empty and regarding it as inhabited by inferior races. One sees this ambivalence in the European description of America, in the Afrikaner description of Southern Africa, and, yes, in the Jewish description of Palestine.[3] Sometimes the native inhabitants of the land are invisible to the conquerors—"a land without people for a people without land," in Herzl's famous apothegm; sometimes they are noticed but scorned. Either way, colonialism entails a denial of respect.

Understanding that the denial of respect may itself constitute the wound that provokes nationalism will enable us in the West to understand what is otherwise so perplexing to us—namely, the fact that over and over in the modern world a people will react against even a relatively enlightened colonialist paternalism and will tolerate as its replacement an authoritarian regime led by one of its own members. It will also help us to understand the response of the blacks to the Afrikaners. Of course the paternalism of the Afrikaners is by no means enlightened. But paternalism it is. The Afrikaners think and speak of the blacks in their midst as children who must carefully—and oh so slowly—be nurtured into adulthood. This is part, but by no means the whole, of the wound they inflict upon the blacks. The Afrikaners are baffled, or say they are baffled, by the fact that these children in their midst do not appreciate all the good things dispensed to them. After all, they say, the blacks have it better in South Africa than anywhere else in Africa. But do they not see that when they treat the blacks as children, they inflict on them a deep wound? Do we not all prefer at some time in our lives to be delivered from the suffocating benefactions of parents and to be on our own—even if that means going hungry for a while and living in cold attics?

Perhaps he exaggerated, yet there was deep truth in what Kant said when he remarked that "paternalism is the greatest despotism imaginable." Better that one be ruled by one's own, even if the rule be harsh and the food be less, than that one's whole people be treated insultingly as children. For now at least one is recognized as a human being. As Berlin remarks in his "Two Concepts of Liberty,"

> I may feel unfree . . . as a member of an unrecognized or insufficiently respected group: then I wish for the emancipation of my entire class, or community, or nation, or race, or profession. So much can I desire this, that I may, in my bitter longing for status, prefer to be bullied and misgoverned by some member of my own race or social class, by whom I am, nevertheless, recognized as a man and a rival—that is as an equal—to being well and tolerantly treated by someone from some higher and remoter group who does not recognize me for what I wish to feel myself to be.[4]

Until we in the West understand these dynamics, until we understand what treating a people paternalistically and not acknowledging their adulthood is itself, apart from whatever else we may do to them, to inflict a deep wound on them, our contemporary world will continue to baffle us.* Of course, the Afrikaners do understand, despite the fact that they prefer to put it out of their mind: they themselves rejected the relatively generous paternalism of the British for the harshness of independence.

A nation may be anywhere along the spectrum from a barely dawning sense of nationhood to an intense conviction of self-importance; the particular form its nationalism takes will depend not only on the nature of that which provokes its self-preoccupation, but also on where it stands along that spectrum. A nation that already has an intense feeling of its own significance will, when it senses that some injury has been done it, have few options apart from either flailing out aggressively so as to right the wrong or at least show that it is not merely a paper tiger, or, alternatively, nursing its wounds in self-pity. The behavior of the United States after the Viet Nam war seems to me a prime example of this form of nationalism. By contrast, the effect of nationalism on a nation that has only a weak sense of nationhood will first of all be to strengthen that sense. One sees this happening among the blacks in South Africa today

*A striking example of the insistence on national self-respect can be found in this passage from a speech of Fidel Castro, in which he criticizes the tendency of some Cubans to rely on socialist aid for rescue whenever hostile countries apply pressure: "Imagine that one day there would be a total blockade, through which no fuel, through which nothing could pass. I am sure, I have absolutely no doubt, that the people would be able to withstand such a situation . . . a situation where fuel would be reserved for the tanks, the lorries, for transporting the army and the armed services. And the population of the cities? We would all move to the country, and work by the side of the farmers, driving the oxen and digging with hoe, pick and shovel. And we would win through. This means that we have the right to hold our heads high, the right to speak our own opinions and ideas; the right to be an example to any of the small countries of the world, to any of the underdeveloped countries dominated by imperialism or colonialism in any part of the world. And this also means that we are committed to gain a place in world history" (speech delivered 2 Jan. 1965, quoted by Denis Goulet, *The Cruel Choice: A New Concept in the Theory of Development* [New York: Atheneum, 1971], p. 46).

and among the Palestinians in the Near East. Indeed, one of the surest ways to intensify a group's feelings of national identity, where those are weak, is to wound the group. If the Palestinians were not a nation, as so many Jewish leaders have insisted, they have certainly become one. And though the blacks of South Africa were many nations, they are well on the way to achieving unity.

The most interesting and also the most common cases, however, are those of wounded nations that fall between these two extremes. If leaders of such a people arise in the time of its sorrows, they will invariably engage first of all in a wide-ranging attempt to build up the nation's self-respect—that is, to increase *pride* in one's identification as a member of the nation and to increase *loyalty* to the nation as such. They will do so by seeking to recover "authentic" elements from the nation's past, by seeking to "purify" the nation's life of "foreign" elements, and by promoting the expansion of this recovered and purified cultural heritage. And they will try to persuade the members of the nation as well as all those looking on from outside that this history and this culture are glorious and worthy. They will sing its praises.[5]

I said: *if* leaders of the people arise in the time of its sorrows; the attainment or recovery of its self-respect is not the automatic response of a nation to a wound. Leaders are needed who have some vision concerning where the glory of the nation lies. But even before those leaders can have such a vision, something else must often happen. When a nation is wounded by being denied self-respect, it characteristically *internalizes that denial.* It comes to believe that it is not *worthy* of self-respect. Its members come to loathe themselves—on account of being black, on account of being native American, on account of being Arab. In that case, what is first of all necessary is that there be leaders who overcome that self-loathing. I think there is nothing more powerful for effecting this step than the conviction that God says to every human being whatsoever: you bear my image. When this word is genuinely heard, self-loathing is no longer possible. And when self-loathing has been overcome, then the next step can occur: something significant and worthy can be seen in the history and culture of one's people.

Afrikanerdom is a paradigm of the intermediate form of nationalism of which I have been speaking. As T. Dunbar Moodie makes clear in his book *The Rise of Afrikanerdom,* the Afrikaners before the twentieth century had no particular sense of self-importance. Indeed, their sense of national identity was not even particularly intense. Today, as the result of more than fifty years of nationalism, the situation is profoundly different. The wound to the people was of course the oppression and cultural humiliation inflicted by the English on the Afrikaner. In the time of its sorrows, the necessary leaders, especially intellectual leaders, arose among the Afrikaner people, and they self-consciously set about raising their people's self-respect. They did so in the classic way, by refining and intensifying the Afrikaners' awareness of their history and culture (including their language), and by singing the glories thereof—in addition, it may be added, to working for Afrikaner self-determination, both cultural and political. The result is an extraordinarily intense loyalty of Afrikaners to their nation and an extraordinarily intense pride in their identification as members of the nation.

I spoke just now about the Afrikaner's struggle for self-determination. It is very nearly inevitable that nationalism, if it does not take the form of a nation licking its wounds, will incorporate a struggle for the nation's right to determine its own form of life on significant points. In its essence, this is a struggle for *cultural* self-determination, yet it invariably has political significance as well. It is true that the struggle need not involve the goal of political *independence,* since it is possible for a nation to enjoy all the cultural self-determination it desires without having political independence, but as we shall shortly see, there are dynamics in the modern world that often thwart that eventuality. And in any case, the political significance of a nation's strengthening sense of nationhood and its rising sense of self-respect is evident to friend and foe alike. It is no accident that in the occupied territories Israel is doing all it can to suppress Palestinian cultural consciousness. It is likewise no accident that the Afrikaner is doing all he can to suppress black cultural consciousness.

Nationalism, I have suggested, is a nation's preoccupation with itself, provoked by its sense of a deficiency in its existence. It is the indication of a nation's perception of itself as diseased or injured. Often the effect of a nationalist episode in a nation's life is that its disease is cured, the pain of its injury salved. Nationalism has then functioned as a restorative antibody, as a healing ointment. Post-colonial nationalism in the Third World was, in good measure, a healing phenomenon.

But sometimes nationalism does not go away. Sometimes the preoccupation of a nation with itself continues beyond the correction of the deficiency in its life. Then we are confronted with something not healing but destructive:

> Original nationalism inspires the people to struggle for what they lack to achieve this. But when nationalism transgresses its lawful limits, when it tries to do more than overcome a deficiency, it becomes guilty of what has been called *hybris* in the lives of historical personalities; it crosses the holy border and grows presumptuous. And now it no longer indicates disease, but is itself a grave and complicated disease. A people can win the rights for which it strove and yet fail to regain its health—because nationalism, turned false, eats at its marrow.[6]

A nation can become so preoccupied with itself that its welfare becomes for its members the sovereign good: "*Deutschland über Alles,*" "America first." Then the actions of the nation are no longer submitted to the requirements of justice and peace. They are no longer submitted to normative appraisal. They are no longer tested against the demands of a sovereign Lord. The nation begins to consider itself sovereign. It treats itself as supreme, as ultimate. Loyalty to nation becomes an end in itself. Pride in membership supersedes all other identifications. Legitimate nationalism has then become idolatrous nationalism—idolatrous in the same way that, as we saw earlier, the pursuit of economic growth can become idolatrous. Idolatrous nationalism is not healthful; it is intensely poisonous. When a nation suffers from nationalism unchecked, the life of its members is twisted and distorted, and the nation becomes a menace among nations because it accepts no standards for international peace and justice. It acts solely in its own self-interest, breaking treaties when it sees fit, waging wars when it finds the advantage, thumbing its nose at international conventions and organizations. National self-assertion is its only goal. All that restrains it is a balance of terror.

For the signs of nationalism gone cancerous, the Christian, and everyone else, must be constantly alert; and when we see the signs, we must do all in our power to check the virulent sickness. We in our century have seen, and continue to see, that there is nothing more destructive of shalom than such nationalism. Of this Martin Buber spoke eloquently—presciently—in his address to the Twelfth Zionist Congress in September, 1921:

> Every reflective member of a people is in duty bound to distinguish between legitimate and arbitrary nationalism and—in the sequence of situations and decisions—to refresh this distinction day after day. This is, above all, an obligation imposed on the leaders of a nation and of national movements.
>
> But the criterion which must govern the drawing of this distinction is not implicit in nationalism itself. It can be found only in the knowledge that the nation has an obligation which is more than merely national. He who regards the nation as the supreme principle, as the ultimate reality, as the final judge, and does not recognize that over and above all the countless and varied peoples there is an authority named or unnamed to which communities as well as individuals must inwardly render an account of themselves, could not possibly know how to draw this distinction, even if he attempted to do so. . . .
>
> He . . . who regards the nation as an end in itself will refuse to admit that there is a greater structure, unless it be the world-wide supremacy of his own particular nation. . . . He does not meet responsibility face to face. He considers the nation its own

> judge and responsible to no one but itself. An interpretation such as this converts the nation into a moloch which gulps the best of the people's youth. . . . All sovereignty becomes false and vain when in the struggle for power it fails to remain subject to the Sovereign of the world, who is the Sovereign of my rival, and my enemy's Sovereign, as well as mine. [7]

That form of nationalism which serves to restore a nation to health can do without explicit articulated justification. Such healing nationalism speaks for itself. Not so with nationalism gone cancerous; for this, an ideology is necessary. The ideology that has characteristically been mustered in support of cancerous nationalism in our modern world was created in the Romantic movement of nineteenth-century Germany. There it was argued, in the first place, that each individual human being belongs to a particular nation whose way of life determines the character and life-purposes of the individual members. Thus the individual cannot be understood apart from his nation. The nation must not be thought of as a group of self-determining individuals, but rather the individuals must be thought of as parts of the self-determining nation. Secondly, it was argued that the best way to think of the relation of parts to parts and of parts to whole in a nation is by analogy to a biological organism: the significance of the individual is fundamentally that, in interaction with others, he or she contributes to the functioning of the whole.*

But the assertion that it is the nation that constitutes the larger whole that defines the character of individuals and demands their contributions begs the question: why should this larger whole not be humanity at large instead? To this the reply of the German Romantics was that the struggle of competing elements is essential to the progress of humanity toward unity. Self-realization is not a smooth, uneventful process, but the outcome of strife and struggle. Kant had already made this point in his treatise *Perpetual Peace*: nature, he said, "employs two means to keep peoples from being mixed and to differentiate them: the difference of *language* and of *religion*. These differences occasion the inclination toward mutual hatred and the excuse for war; yet at the same time they lead, as culture increases and men gradually come closer together, toward

*The idea of an organism, says Fichte, "has been used lately with frequency in order to define the different branches of the public authority in its unity; but not yet, so far as I know, to explain the totality of civil relations. In a product of nature, no part is what it is but through its relation with the whole, and would absolutely not be what it is apart from this relation . . .; similarly, man attains a determinate position in the scheme of things and fixity in nature only by means of civil association. . . . Between the isolated man and the citizen, there is the same relation as between raw and organized matter. . . . In an organized body, each part continuously maintains the whole, and in maintaining it, maintains itself also. Similarly, the citizen with regard to the state" (quoted by Elie Kedouri, *Nationalism,* 2d ed. rev. [New York: Praeger, 1961], pp. 39–40).

a greater agreement on principles for peace and understanding." [8] The progress of civilization and the attainment of ultimate harmony demand distinct peoples in competition with each other.

The contention that the struggle of nation with nation is essential to historical advance has consistently been coupled with a fourth theme—the importance of diversity among nations. Writers such as Schleiermacher viewed each nation as a natural division of humanity, having a peculiar character which it is the duty of its members to preserve and enhance: "Every nationality," he says, "is destined through its peculiar organization and its place in the world to represent a certain side of the divine image. . . . For it is God who directly assigns to each nationality its definite task on earth and inspires it with a definite spirit in order to glorify himself through each one in a peculiar manner." [9]

The conclusion drawn by the nineteenth-century German theorists from the interweaving of these four themes of self-determination, organicism, struggle, and diversity was that nations are separate natural entities ordained by God, in loyalty to which individuals find the meaning of their lives, and that the right political arrangement is one in which each nation is self-determining. Only in such an arrangement, they said, would the peoples of the earth fulfill their unique destinies, each making its particular contribution to the whole, and only by sinking themselves into the greater whole of their nation would individuals find freedom and fulfillment; furthermore, the struggle resulting from an international order thus arranged would advance the cause of humanity. It was this ideology that was self-consciously imported into South Africa by the Afrikaner intellectuals in the early part of this century. They adapted it to the South African situation by arguing that it had an Old Testament basis and that one of the defining features of the Afrikaner *volk* is that its religion is Christianity. What has emerged is a strange amalgam that the Afrikaners themselves call *Christian nationalism*.

I have been offering a general account of nationalism, and along the way I have indicated how this general account fits certain specific cases, including the United States. Yet there are also important peculiarities in the case of the United States, and before we move on to some of the ways in which nations interact with states and with the economic order in our present world-system, we might consider some of these peculiarities. We can approach the matter by asking why contemporary American intellectuals are so reluctant to sing the glories of their nation's history and culture. The Afrikaner intellectuals have not hesitated to bend their efforts toward the advancement of their nation and to hymn the glories of its accomplishments. And up through the first quarter of this century the American intellectuals readily did the same for their country. But now, silence—or even bitter attack. Why so?

Well, for one thing, what can the intellectual do? Undoubtedly

America feels wounded by the experiences of the last decade, but there is here no weak sense of nationhood. Nor does America have an insufficiently developed sense of its unique significance in the history of mankind which the scholar can then work to overcome. If anything, its sense of significance has for a long time been inflated. Consider, for example, these words spoken in the first decade of this century, not by some odd crank, but by William Rainey Harper, the noted Old Testament scholar who became the first president of the University of Chicago:

> Another great period is just being ushered in, which promises to eclipse its predecessor even as that predecessor eclipsed those that preceded it. . . . What Babylonia was in the first period, what Syria was in the second, what England was in the third, all this and more America will be in the fourth. . . .
>
> [The] idea of individualism, of the paramount dignity of the individual, has expressed itself, more clearly and more specifically, in every advance of civilization. . . .
>
> But, now, these ideas have been demonstrated only "piecemeal, and incoherently, in separated times and places." However clearly they may have been taught in the New Testament, they have not yet received their perfect demonstration in human history. The question of individualism as a whole is still on trial. . . . The arena in which the great trial shall be conducted is America. The old countries with their traditions and institutions which obstruct their performance of full human functions by the masses, cannot work out the problems which confront us.
>
> . . . Here in this great country, provided by God himself with all the facilities needed, preserved in large measure by God himself from the burdens and trammels of dead institutions and deadly traditions, the consummation of Christian life and thought will be realized. This is the message written on every page of our nineteen centuries of history. It is a wonderful and significant message.
>
> . . . If, now, our faith is sure that there has been committed to us this great mission, shall we not purify ourselves? Shall we not organize ourselves as a nation for the work that lies ahead?[10]

This flamboyant expression of American importance should by no means be seen as merely an expression of Harper's personal opinion. When these words were spoken, almost all Americans would in substance have agreed with them. Many still would. And let us recall that the sense of national self-importance to which Harper was giving expression had been carefully nursed and promoted by American intellectuals throughout the eighteenth and nineteenth centuries. I submit that when a nation with this highly developed sense of self-importance feels wounded, there is little that the intellectuals can do to restore its sense of self-respect—other than to persuade it that it need not feel wounded. They have already done all they could.

But to understand fully the alienation and anger of contemporary American intellectuals, one must also consider the peculiar character of their nation's sense of self-importance. From the eighteenth century on, America's sense of self-importance has always been connected to the understanding it has of its relationship to those great universalistic Enlightenment goals of liberty, equality, and fraternity. Americans insisted that it was in this land that those great ideals were first being realized, and that from this land they would spread throughout the world. America was not just a nation among nations, not even just a *significant* nation among nations. In America was being created a new nation out of fragments of many nations to be a model for all nations. The Romantic ideology with its emphasis on the unique contribution of each nation never enjoyed favor among Americans. America was every nation's future. And part of its frustration during the past fifty years is that it finds itself in the world with another social group whose leaders believe a similar destiny has been entrusted to their nation—namely, the Soviet Union.

Our world today is a world of failed ideals. Not many Russians believe that in their land a new age of equality and participation is being ushered in. No longer do many Americans believe that in their land a new age of liberty and equality has arrived. The diplomats of America now pursue a policy exclusively of self-interest. It bothers them little that self-interest requires the support of regimes around the world that suppress liberty. For a brief period during the Carter administration there was talk of America being the protector of human rights around the globe. That brief flash has vanished into the dark night of shoring up business interests and opposing communism.

I suggest that when the intellectuals in a nation or group once inspired by this peculiar sense of universalistic importance are confronted by failed ideals, by the reality that their group is no longer an effective, devoted agent of those universalistic goals, they will become alienated. Most will convey their alienation in expressions of diminished loyalty: a few will resort to bitter attacks. A few neo-conservatives only will shout shrilly that the glories of the group are as great as ever, that the ideals have not failed, but that disloyal people only *say* they have.

It is time to return to the contention with which I opened this chapter: if we probe into the *causes* of the deprivation of rights and the perpetuation of misery in the modern world, again and again we shall find excessive and misguided loyalty to nation at work. When nationalism produces a morbid preoccupation of a nation with itself, it is bad enough, but when it produces a loyalty that considers the existence and aggrandizement of the nation to be the ultimate social good, then we are dealing with an idolatry that is enormously destructive of shalom. Sometimes this loyalty manifests itself in the aggressive, self-interested, terroristic treament by one state of other states and their citizens. Sometimes it manifests itself internally in the way in which the state treats its own citizens. I do not know which of these manifestations is more injurious, but to give some indication of how loyalty to nation produces injustice, let me focus on the second.

It is often said that characteristic of the political composition of the modern world is the fact that states are nation-states. Surely that is false if the suggestion is being made that the citizenry of most states belong to a single nation; rather, what is true is that the world is now constituted by those tightly defined entities that are our modern states and that one of the most important factors accounting for the differentiation of these states is the insistence of nations that they have a state of their own. Of course, nations have always struggled for *cultural* self-determination; what is peculiar to the modern world is the degree to which nations have struggled for *political* self-determination—and the degree to which those struggles have been successful. The principle of *each nation its own state* has come to seem obviously correct as a principle for assigning sovereignty. At Versailles the old political map of Europe was torn apart and pasted together again on this principle.

I suggest, however, that if we allow our reflections on this principle to go beyond its initial attractiveness, we shall be forced to the conclusion that never in the modern world is it acceptable, inasmuch as it always leads to injustice and conflict. The crux of what goes wrong is that states are of course territorial entities, and nowhere in the modern world are the inhabitants of the territory belonging to a state the members of just one nation. Consequently, when one nation has a state of its own, there will nevertheless always be citizens of that state who are not members of the nation, and these people will be left with only two choices: either to emigrate, under varying degrees of duress, or to accept the status of second-class citizens, with varying degrees of deprivation of rights and of repression. *There is never any other choice.*

The insistence of the Afrikaners that they have a state of their own—along with their insistence that whether they like it or not the black tribes shall also (eventually) have states of their own—lies at the bottom of the grievous injustices that the South African state wreaks on the blacks. The dynamic behind apartheid is not racism in a straightforward way; it is cancerous nationalism (though indeed a racist species of that): loyalty to nation supersedes all. This loyalty leads the Afrikaner to embrace the principle of *my nation its own state,* and to this principle the requirements of justice and peace are subordinated. The actions of the state are judged by whether they serve the cause of the Afrikaner people, not by whether they serve the cause of justice.

In public Afrikaners will often insist that the legal structure of apartheid is not some ultimate good, but that it is in principle only a dispensable *means.* What they have in mind when they say this, however, is not that the structure of apartheid is the means for achieving a society of *justice,* but that it is the means for achieving the goal of *my nation its own state*—and, more generally, for the goal of the *self-determination of the Afrikaner people.* They cannot conceive of the social good as not including the full self-determination of their own people: their *nation,* not justice, is the ultimate social commitment. The speeches they make to their compatriots in private make this clear. In 1970 Dr. Piet Meyer, chairman of the Broederbond, had this to say: "We must never accede to any demands to scrap or water down our policy of separate development and anti-communism . . . All forms of integration in our country must be fought and rejected on all fronts—in the churches, and in the social, cultural, economic and political spheres."[11] And in 1975 the Executive of the Bond said that "measures necessary to keep political control of the white man's future in his own hands must not disappear. Thus no form of political power-sharing with non-white nations is acceptable."[12] I submit, however, that in a multinational and economically integrated society such as South Africa, the principle of *the Afrikaners their own state* is incompatible with the demands of peace and justice.

A nation may have "its own state" in many different ways. In South Africa we see one form of ethnic state. Since the blacks are a large majority there, the centerpiece of Afrikaner policy is to deprive them of all voice in the affairs of state and to force as many as possible into homelands. In Israel we see a different form of ethnic state. For one thing, in Israel proper, Palestinian Arabs are allowed to vote. Yet Israel is a Jewish state. And if we ask what it is that accounts for the injustices that Israel has wreaked and continues to wreak on the Arabs, the conclusion is inescapable that it is in good measure the principle of *the Jewish nation its own state.**

Zionism arose in the context of nineteenth-century European nationalism. The Israeli editor Gershom Schocken has remarked that "Zionism

*There are other factors to be considered concerning the Israeli treatment of the Palestinian Arabs as well. As early as 1891—fifty-seven years before the Jewish people had acquired their own state—the well-known Jewish writer Ahad Ha-am warned that the Jewish settlers ought not to arouse the wrath of the natives with ugly actions, but ought instead to meet them in the friendly spirit of respect. "Yet what," he asked, "do our brethren do in Palestine? Just the opposite! Serfs they were in the lands of the diaspora and suddenly they find themselves in freedom, and this change has awakened in them an inclination to despotism. They treat the Arabs with hostility and cruelty, deprive them of their rights, offend them without cause, and even boast of these deeds; and nobody among us opposes this despicable and dangerous inclination" (quoted by Hans Kohn, "Zion and the Jewish National Idea," in *Zionism Reconsidered: The Rejection of Jewish Normalcy,* ed. Michael Selzer [New York: Macmillan, 1970], p. 195).

could not have arisen without the national movements which altered the face of Europe during the nineteenth century, without the discovery by the Russian *narodniki* of the spiritual wealth of the simple people and their needs and problems, and without German romanticism. Kurt Blumenfeld, the important ideologue of German Zionism, said with good reason: Zionism is the gift of Europe to the Jewish people."[13] Having imbibed the spirit of European nationalism, the Zionist claimed that since the Jews are a distinct people, and since every people is entitled to its own land and its own state, the Jews are so entitled as well. Already in 1900 an orthodox rabbi of Eastern Europe lodged a bitter attack on Zionism on the ground of its being inspired by nationalism and not by Judaism. "For our many sins," wrote the rabbi,

> strangers have risen to pasture the holy flock, men who say that the people of Israel should be clothed in secular nationalism, a nation like all other nations, that Judaism rests on three things, national feeling, the land and the language, and that national feeling is the most praiseworthy element in the brew and the most effective in preserving Judaism, while the observance of the Torah and the commandments is a private matter depending on the inclination of each individual. May the Lord rebuke these evil men and may he who chooseth Jerusalem seal their mouths.[14]

Of course the early Zionist leaders did not merely stake their case on the claim that the Jews constitute a distinct people and as such deserve their own state; they also undertook to point out the evil consequences of violating the principle of each nation its own state in this case—or, conversely, the advantages of respecting it: only by granting the Jews their own state, they argued, could the "Jewish problem"—that is, rampant anti-Semitism—be solved (and let me just say here that this widespread virulent hatred and discrimination against Jews remains an important issue today). In addition, they argued that only by granting the Jews their own state could "the problem of Judaism"—that is, the problem of the erosion of Jewish identity—be solved. The alliance of Zionism with European nationalism enabled its leaders on the one hand to combat the modernists, who expected the progress of emancipation and enlightenment to solve "the Jewish problem," but who had no answer to "the problem of Judaism"; and on the other hand, it allowed them to combat the traditionalists, who saw the preservation of their traditional enclaves as the solution to "the problem of Judaism," but who had no solution to "the Jewish problem."

To understand fully how the principle of *the Jews their own state* has worked itself out in Palestine, we must add one more thing: the fact that the Jewish leaders have traditionally seen the Jewish people as the *only* nation in Palestine. In this way they differ from the Afrikaners, who see themselves as dwelling with many other nations on the tip of Africa. The Palestinians, insists the Jew, do not constitute a people. It was this insistence that lay behind these remarkable words of Golda Meir:

> How can we return the occupied territories? There is nobody to return them to. . . . There was no such thing as Palestinians. . . . It was not as though there was a Palestinian people in Palestine considering itself as a Palestinian people and we came and threw them out and took their country away from them. They did not exist.[15]

Meir knew, of course, that there had been Arabs living in Palestine before the formation of the Israeli state, and she knew very well that they had been dispossessed of their land, but they were not a people in her view, and so consequently she saw no substantial issue of rights. That there are human beings with blood that runs and tears that flow among nations other than one's own is scarcely visible to the person blinded by nationalism.

In his book *Zionism and the Palestinians,* Simha Flapan traces in detail the attitudes of the Jewish leaders toward the Arabs living in Palestine. Few indeed there were who sought in Palestine anything other than a state of their own for the Jewish people; and of that large majority who sought an ethnic state, only Dr. Nahum Goldmann among the top Zionist leadership saw clearly that a state of their own for the Jews raised profound issues concerning the rights of the Palestinians. "One of the great oversights," Goldmann said on one occasion,

> in the history of Zionism is that when the Jewish homeland in Palestine was founded, sufficient attention was not paid to relations with the Arabs. Of course, there were always a few Zionist speakers and thinkers who stressed them. . . . And the ideological and political leaders of the Zionist movement always emphasized—sincerely and earnestly, it seems to me—that the Jewish national home must be established in peace and harmony with the Arabs. Unfortunately these convictions remained in the realm of theory and were not carried over, to any great extent, into actual Zionist practice. Even Theodor Herzl's brilliantly simple formulation of the Jewish question as basically a transportation problem of 'moving people without a home into a land without a people' is tinged with disquieting blindness to the Arab claim to Palestine. Palestine was not a land without a people even in Herzl's time; it was inhabited by hundreds of thousands of Arabs who, in the course of events, would sooner or later have achieved independent statehood, either alone or as a unit with a larger Arab context.[16]

Goldmann's awareness of the existence of an emerging Palestinian people did not carry the day. Instead, Zionist and Israeli policy was determined by such individuals as David Ben-Gurion, who remarked in 1936 that "there is no conflict between Jewish and Palestinian nationalism because the Jewish nation is not in Palestine and the Palestinians are not a nation."[17] The standard view of the Zionist leaders has always been that although there is an Arab people, there is no Palestinian people, and that since Palestine constitutes only a bit more than two percent of the total area occupied by the Arabs in the Near East, there is no good reason why they should not be willing to give up that small part of their territory to the Jews, who need it more than the Arabs do, and who will use it better.[18] It is the legacy and perpetuation of these attitudes that feed the Palestinians' justified sense of grievance.

The die was cast in 1944, when the American Zionists, the largest section of the World Zionist Organization, unanimously resolved to demand a "free and democratic Jewish commonwealth . . . [which] shall embrace the whole of Palestine, undivided and undiminished."[19] A *Jewish* commonwealth. An ethnic state. The result for the Arabs has been what it always is in our modern world when one nation claims a state for its own: they could either emigrate from their ancestral homes under some form of duress or be demoted to second-class citizenship that would be enforced with some degree of repression. *There is never any other choice.* Let me allow a member of the Jewish people, one of the fathers of Zionism, make the point. In 1953 Moshe Smilansky, in response to the Israeli parliament's passage of the "Land Requisition Law of 1953," made this statement:

> When we came back to our country after having been evicted two thousand years ago, we called ourselves "daring" and we rightly complained before the whole world that the gates of the country were shut. And now when they [Arab refugees] dared to return to their country where they lived for one thousand years before they were evicted or fled, they are called "infiltrees" and shot in cold blood. Where are you, Jews? Why do we not at least, with a generous hand, pay compensation to these miserable people? Where to take the money from? But we build palaces . . . instead of paying a debt that cries unto us from earth and heaven. . . . And do we sin only against the refugees? Do we not treat the Arabs who remain with us as second-class citizens? . . . Did a single Jewish farmer raise his hand in the parliament in opposition to a law that deprived Arab peasants of their land? . . . How does sit solitary, in the city of Jerusalem, the Jewish conscience![20]

We have looked at just two cases, but the point has been made: it is justice and shalom that determine the legitimacy of a state, not the principle of national self-determination. Does the state protect the rights of those who dwell there? Does it deal equitably with them? Does it establish peace? Those are the questions to be asked, not whether some nation has its own state. Nation must bow before justice. A state is to be the state of *all* its citizens, not the state of some nation *among* its citizens.[21] What unites us as bearers of the image of God is more important than what divides us as members of nations. In their dispensing of justice, the states of the world must always make their ethnic diversity secondary to their essential human unity rather than the other way around. In the modern world this means that there can be no ethnic state, because such a state inevitably wreaks injustice. The evidence is all about us; as George Orwell once remarked, "The nationalist not only does not disapprove of atrocities committed by his own side, but he has a remarkable capacity for not even hearing about them."[22]

As Christians struggle to diminish the conflict of nation against nation in the world today they will not forget the life of that other nation to which they belong, that "holy nation," in Peter's words, the church of Jesus Christ—"elect from every nation, yet one o'er all the earth." After Pentecost God's chosen people on earth no longer excludes the members of any natural grouping—neither Greek nor Jew, female nor male, slave nor free. It does not exclude them because it transcends them. Without destroying all those old loyalties, it transforms them: they become enrichments of this one new nation. So at least it was meant to be. And here and there, now and then, that is how it is. Yet in the modern world, loyalty to nation has bitten so deeply into the life of the church that most Christians in America feel themselves less united as members of one holy dedicated nation with those in Russia, in Vietnam, in Germany, or in El Salvador than they feel themselves divided from them as Americans in distinction from Russians, from Vietnamese, from Germans, from Salvadorans. And so American bombs are dropped by Christians on the cathedral in Hanoi just as German bombs were dropped by Christians on the churches in Rotterdam.

Can that change? Can the church live up to its inner nature? Can it become consistently a sacrament, an effective sign of God's Kingdom of shalom in which no longer shall a nation build but not inhabit, plant but not eat (Isa. 65:22)? For in that Kingdom "nation shall not lift up sword against nation, / neither shall they learn war any more" (Isa. 2:4).

Notes

[1] Ibid., p. 346.

[2] Buber, *Israel,* p. 218.

[3] For a confirmation of this claim in the case of the Jews and Palestine, see Edward Said's *The Question of Palestine* (New York: Vintage Books, 1980).

[4] Berlin, "Two Concepts of Liberty," in *Four Essays on Liberty* (New York: Oxford University Press, 1970), p. 157.

[5] On this, see Karl Deutsch's *Tides among Nations* (New York: Free Press, 1979), p. 29.

[6] Buber, *Israel,* p. 219.

[7] Ibid., pp. 220–24.

[8] Kant, "Eternal Peace," in *The Philosophy of Kant: Immanuel Kant's Moral and Political Writings* trans. and ed. Carl J. Friedrich (New York: Modern Library, 1949), p. 454.

[9] Schleiermacher, quoted by Kedouri, *Nationalism,* p. 58.

[10] Harper, *Religion and the Higher Life: Talks to Students* (Chicago: University of Chicago Press, 1904), pp. 174–80.

[11] Meyer, quoted by Ivor Wilkins and Hans Strydom, *The Broederbond* (New York: Paddington Press, 1979), p. 203.

[12] Ibid., p. 209.

[13] Schocken, "Revisiting Zionism," *New York Review of Books,* 28 May 1981, p. 42. For an excellent survey of the relation of Zionism to nationalism, see Kohn, "Zion and the Jewish National Idea," in *Zionism Reconsidered: The Rejection of Jewish Normalcy,* ed. Michael Selzer (New York: Macmillan, 1970), pp. 175–212.

[14] Quoted by Elie Kedouri, *Nationalism,* 2d ed. rev. (New York: Praeger, 1961), p. 76.

[15] Meir, quoted by Frank H. Epp, *Whose Land Is Palestine?: The Middle East Problem in Historical Perspective* (Grand Rapids, Mich.: Eerdmans, 1970), p. 253.

[16] Goldmann, *Memories: The Autobiography of Nahum Goldmann* (London: Weidenfeld and Nicholson, 1970), p. 284.

[17] Ben-Gurion, quoted by Simha Flapan, *Zionism and the Palestinians* (New York: Barnes & Noble, 1979), p. 131.

[18] See Flapan, *Zionism and the Palestinians,* p. 135.

[19] Hannah Arendt had this to say concerning the event: "The end result of fifty years of Zionist politics was embodied in the recent resolution of the largest and most influential section of the World Zionist Organization. American Zionists from left to right adopted unanimously, at their last annual convention held in Atlantic City in October, 1944, the demand for a 'free and democratic Jewish commonwealth . . . [which] shall embrace the whole of Palestine, undivided and undiminished.' This is a turning-point in Zionist history; for it means that the Revisionist program, so long bitterly repudiated, has proved finally victorious. The Atlantic City Resolution goes even a step further than the Biltmore Program (1942), in which the Jewish minority had granted minority rights to the Arab majority. This time the Arabs were simply not mentioned in the resolution, which obviously leaves them the choice between voluntary emigration or second-class citizenship" ("Zionism Reconsidered," in *Zionism Reconsidered,* p. 213).

[20] Smilansky, quoted by Kohn, "Zion and the Jewish National Idea," in *Zionism Reconsidered,* p. 206.

[21] Regarding this issue, consider these words of Ahad Ha-am, writing in sorrow to his people late in life that the historical right of the Jews in Palestine "does not affect the right of the other inhabitants who are entitled to invoke the right of actual dwelling and their work in the country for many generations. For them, too, the country is a national home, and they have a right to develop national forces to the extent of their ability. This situation makes Palestine the common land of several peoples, each of whom wishes to build its national home there. In such circumstances it is no longer possible that the national home of one of them could be total. . . . If you build your house not in an empty space, but in a place where there are also other houses and inhabitants, you are unrestricted master only inside your own house. Outside the door all the inhabitants are partners, and the management of the whole has to be directed in agreement with the interests of them all" (from *At the Crossroads* [1920], quoted by Kohn, "Zion and the Jewish National Idea," in *Zionism Reconsidered,* p. 202).

[25] Orwell, "Notes on Nationalism," in *The Collected Essays, Journalism and Letters of George Orwell* (New York: Harcourt, Brace & World, 1968), vol. 3, *As I Please: 1943-1945,* p. 370.

Appendices

Appendix A

Chicago Sun-Times, Wednesday, Nov. 9, 1977 68

ADVERTISEMENT ADVERTISEMENT ADVERTISEMENT ADVERTISEMENT ADVERTISEMENT

EVANGELICALS' CONCERN FOR ISRAEL

HOLY BIBLE

We the undersigned *Evangelical Christians* affirm our belief in the right of Israel to exist as a free and independent nation and in this light we voice our grave apprehension concerning the recent direction of American foreign policy vis a vis the Middle East.

We are particularly troubled by the erosion of American governmental support for Israel evident in the joint U.S.-U.S.S.R. statement.

While we are sympathetic to the human needs of all the peoples of the Middle East, mindful that promises were made to the other descendants of Abraham and concerned about the welfare of Christians in all the countries of the Middle East, we affirm as Evangelicals our belief in the promise of the land to the Jewish people—a promise first made to Abraham and repeated throughout Scripture, a promise which has never been abrogated.

We believe the rebirth of Israel as a nation and the return of her people to the land is clearly foretold in the Bible and this fulfillment in our time is one of the most momentous events in all human history.

While the exact boundaries of the land of promise are open to discussion, we, along with most evangelicals, understand the Jewish homeland generally to include the territory west of the Jordan River.

It should be remembered that from the time of Joshua, this land mass has been the exclusive homeland for the Jewish nation. Jerusalem has never been the capital for any other people since the time of David.

We pray for peace in the Middle East and we pledge ourselves to work for justice for all of the peoples involved yet we also declare our belief that lasting peace cannot be achieved until the international community accepts the inalienable right of the Jewish people to live and create a nation within the boundaries of their ancient homeland.

Further, from the perspective of Israel's security requirements as well as from our understanding of her legacy, **we would view with grave concern any effort to carve out of the historic Jewish homeland another nation or political entity, particularly one which would be governed by terrorists whose stated goal is the destruction of the Jewish state.**

As Evangelicals we are convinced that Israel's future should not and will not be determined by political intrigue, fluctuating world opinion or the imposition of world powers. Rather, we put our trust in the eternality of the covenant God made with Abraham and we find comfort in the words of the prophet Amos—

> *"And I will plant them upon the land and they shall no more be pulled up out of the land which I have given them, saith the Lord, thy God."* Amos 9:15

The time has come for Evangelical Christians to affirm their belief in biblical prophecy and Israel's Divine Right to the Land by speaking out now.

Here's what you can do:

- **Pray for the Peace of Jerusalem.**
- **Write a letter or add your name to this letter and send it to your Government leaders today indicating your support for Israel.**
- **Place this statement in your local newspapers.**

Hudson T. Armerding
Past President, National Association of Evangelicals
Wheaton, Illinois

Pat Boone
Los Angeles, California

W. A. Criswell
Pastor, First Baptist Church
Dallas, Texas

Paul N. Ellis
Bishop, President, Board of Administration
Free Methodist Church of North America
Winona Lake, Indiana

Harry L. Evans
President, Trinity College
Deerfield, Illinois

George Giacumakis, Jr.
Professor of History, California State University
Fullerton, California
and President Elect, Institute of Holy Land Studies
Jerusalem, Israel

Vernon Grounds
President, Conservative Baptist Seminary
Denver, Colorado

Kenneth Kantzer
Vice President, Graduate Studies and
Dean of Trinity Evangelical Divinity School
Deerfield, Illinois

Harold Lindsell
Editor, Christianity Today
Wheaton, Illinois

Kenneth M. Meyer
President, Trinity Evangelical Divinity School
Deerfield, Illinois

Arnold T. Olson, *Coordinator*
President Emeritus, Evangelical Free
Church of America
Past President, National Association of Evangelicals
Minneapolis, Minnesota

B. Elmo Scoggin
Professor, Hebrew and Old Testament
Southeastern Baptist Seminary
Wake Forest, North Carolina

Clyde Taylor
General Director, National Association
of Evangelicals (retired)
Arnold, Maryland

John F. Walvoord
President, Dallas Theological Seminary
Dallas, Texas

G. Douglas Young
President, Institute of Holy Land Studies
Jerusalem, Israel

ORGANIZATIONS LISTED FOR PURPOSES OF IDENTIFICATION ONLY

For further information write to: ARNOLD T. OLSON, Box 19092 Minneapolis, MN 55419

Appendix B

DECLARATION OF THE INTERNATIONAL CHRISTIAN ZIONIST LEADERSHIP CONGRESS
Basel, Switzerland — August 27-29, 1985

Preamble
We delegates, gathered here from many different nations and church backgrounds, in the very same hall where 88 years ago, Dr. Theodor Herzl and the assembled delegates of the first Zionist Congress, laid the foundation for the re-birth of the State of Israel, have come together to pray and seek the Lord, to acknowledge our tremendous debt to Israel (the People, the Land and the Faith) and to show solidarity with her. We realize that today, after the terrible suffering the Jews have experienced, they still face similar hateful and destructive forces.

As Christians we realize that the Church too often failed the Jews in their long history of suffering and persecution. We unite here in Europe, 40 years after the end of the Holocaust, to show our support and to speak up for the state whose birth was prepared here. We say "Never again" to the forces which would bring a new holocaust upon the Jewish People.

First, we speak to our fellow Christians: Let us divest ourselves of any pride or anti-semitism, hidden or open, toward the Jews. Then let us support the Jewish People with heartfelt love, faith and action, in light of what the Bible teaches on God's eternal covenant with His People and His Land.

Second, we congratulate the State of Israel and her citizens for their many achievements in the short span of less than four decades. We exhort you to be strong in the Lord and in the power of His might as you face the many obstacles ahead. We also lovingly implore you: please try to realize more clearly and to acknowledge more openly that it is the hand of God, as prophesied in your Holy Scriptures, which has restored the Land and gathered in the Exiles, not just the strength of your own hands. Finally, we call upon every Jew throughout the world to consider making aliyah to Israel, and upon every Christian to encourage and support their Jewish friends in this freely-taken but God-inspired step.

Third, we speak to the nations which are friends of Israel but whose policies totter between true support and political expediency. We ask you to establish your embassies in Jerusalem, to emphasize the age-old link of the eternal Jewish People with their God-given city, and to recognize Judea and Samaria as part of the Land.

Fourth, we warn the nations hostile to Israel, including the Arab nations (except Egypt) and the Soviet Union, to stop the obstruction of peace in the Middle East.

We also ask the U.S.S.R. to let all Soviet Jews emigrate to Israel, starting with the 400,000 who have requested exit visas, without any further delay, and to grant full religious liberty to all Soviet citizens.

Fifth, we ask nations which have not done so, to recognize Israel diplomatically, to support her internationally, and to oppose any blacklist or boycott against her.

Sixth, most importantly and urgently, we pray for the coming of the day when all peoples in Israel, throughout the Middle East and around the world, truly will live in peace and safety as the Lord has prophesied.

Seventh, we hereby formally adopt the following resolutions of the Congress, and the full text of each which follows:

Res. 1 No Concessions to the U.S.S.R. while Soviet Jews Cannot Emigrate to Israel
Res. 2 Israel Must Reach Out and be Accepted Internationally
Res. 3 All Nations Should Recognize Israel
Res. 4 All Nations Should Recognize Judea and Samaria as Belonging to Israel
Res. 5 All Nations Should Move Their Embassies to Jerusalem
Res. 6 All Friendly Nations Should Desist from Arming Israel's Foes
Res. 7 All Governments Must Stop Entertaining Terrorists
Res. 8 We Condemn Anti-Semitism in all its Forms
Res. 9 We Remember Past Anti-Jewish Atrocities and Resolve "Never Again"
Res. 10 We Encourage Resettlement of the Refugees from Israel and Seek Justice for Jewish Refugees
Res. 11 Let us Help Israel Economically and Create an International Investment Fund
Res. 12 All Nations Should Bar Compliance with Anti-Israel Boycotts
Res. 13 We Call Upon the W.C.C. to see Biblical Link of the People and the Land
Res. 14 We Pray for the Coming Kingdom of the Lord

Appendix C

Mike Evans—Heads Mike Evans Ministries, which is based in Bedford, Texas. Although his mother came from an Orthodox Jewish background, he attended a Christian Bible school as a child. In 1970 he began what he calls "a ministry for Israel;" Mike Evans Ministries is described as an "intercessory arm to the nation of Israel." Evans, a reborn, charismatic Christian, has produced two television specials: "Israel: America's Key to Survival" and "Jerusalem DC [David's Capital]."

He believes that if America fails to accept prophetic responsibilities, America could lose the blessing of God as a result of disobedience. He also claims that there is a Satanic conspiracy behind a fanatical quest by the Muslims to crush Israel and America.

In a 1983 newletter, Evans states: "I believe if America stood up and boldy made a strategic commitment to the State of Israel, recognizing Jerusalem as its capital, that not only would it stop the Soviet Union in its tracks, but put a stop to the enormous amount of Arab blackmail and terrorism—which is absolutely destroying South and Central America."

Mike Evans has met numerous times with former Israeli Prime Minister Menachem Begin, and he prayed with Begin 24 hours before the Israeli invasion of Lebanon.

Evans current focus is on Jerusalem, which he believes must be the undivided capital of Israel. His TV special, "Jerusalem DC," is a plea for money and for signers of a declaration, to be sent to the Prime Minister of Israel and to the President of the United States. This declaration recognizes Jerusalem as Israel's spiritual capital, states support for the people of Israel in their fight for freedom, and says that God will bless those that bless Israel and curse those that curse Israel.

This hour long special features such supporters of Israel as Pat Robertson, Jerry Falwell, Jimmy Swaggert, Pat Boone, Hal Lindsey, Jack Anderson and others. The Palestinians as a people are never mentioned, however there are references to "terrorists," "sinister forces" and "demonic conspiracies" throughout the show. We are told that a "daring pre-emptive strike" on 5 June 1967 changed the course of history. Jerusalem was finally reclaimed by Israel—and the Wailing Wall, which was a garbage dump, becomes a holy place again.

Evans states that it will cost the lives of our own sons and fathers if we don't recognize Jerusalem, and we are told again and again that God will bless those that bless Israel and curse those that curse Israel.

November 19, 1984

Dear Lover of Israel,

I'm enclosing your Proclamation of Jerusalem.

As soon as you let me know you have signed your name to this prophetic document, I will send you a beautiful seal so you can frame your proclamation for all to see.

This is the same Proclamation that I offered on JERUSALEM, D.C., the historic program that aired by satellite from Jerusalem in October and was viewed by millions of people.

I will be presenting this Proclamation of Jerusalem and the names of all those who sign it to the President of the United States and to the Prime Minister of Israel. I'm praying God will lead at least one million people to sign this document within the next few months.

When God laid JERUSALEM, D.C. on my heart, I was fearful because I knew the cost would be tremendous and we just did not have the funds. But I also knew we must stand by Israel during this critical time in history.

My friend, praise God, your prayers and gifts have made the first two legs of this mammoth project a success. The production costs and the satellite airing costs have been paid in full.

Now we are facing the final leg of the entire project and it will be the most expensive by far. God has told me to go deep into the devil's territory and air JERUSALEM, D.C. on prime time television.

But I need your prayerful and financial help as never before because I have stepped out by faith and bought air time all across America.

By buying time on TV stations that air so much of Satan's material we, in essence, are entering his domain. And he is throwing up obstacles to keep JERUSALEM, D.C. from reaching the people.

(FROM A THREE PAGE MIKE EVANS MAILING, November 19, 1984)

AMERICA MUST STAND WITH ISRAEL THE BEAR FROM THE NORTH WILL MAKE ANOTHER MAJOR PRE-ARMAGEDDON ATTEMPT IN '83

Last month I shared with you that the Soviet Union is deploying the biggest military buildup in the history of the Middle East, with almost 500,000 troops either on active or reserve duty. The Soviet Union is less than 900 miles from the main oil fields, while the U.S. is 9,000 miles by air, and if we wanted to move one division of 25,000 troops in, supporting them with 70,000 tons of equipment, it would take us four weeks using all U.S. airlift capabilities.

If America does not stand with Israel, the Soviet Union will overthrow Saudia Arabia and spark a Moslem revolution which could collapse the economies of Europe and Asia.

As you well know, I have provided information to the most famous columnist in America, Jack Anderson, on four occasions. The most historic interview I was given exclusively was between Begin and Sadat before Sadat's assassination, in which Sadat told Begin that Saudia Arabia was the most unstable regime in the Middle East and the Soviet Union had a strategy to overthrow it.

I believe God is calling us to produce this television special to share the truth with our nation and to call one million Christians to intercessory prayer which can and will—by God's grace—turn the tide. Without interceding Christians and a bold attack against Satan like we are attempting, this is what we may have to look forward to:

1. A major move by the Soviet Union from Afghanistan down around the Iran/Pakistan border to the port called Hormuz in the Persian Gulf.
2. I also believe that in '83 Libya may make its move. It has 14 billion dollars worth of Soviet equipment. The Soviets had one of the greatest stockpiles in Lebanon in the history of the world, and the U.S. press never once came out against them . . . only against Israel . . . giving the Soviet Union the green flag, totally convincing them they can make a major move in '83 and have nothing to fear from the international community . . .

Friends, General David C. Jones, Chairman of the Joint Chiefs of Staff, declared, "The United States must get into the Middle East in a hurry. We must make the Soviet Union push us out, rather than push them out." From all indications, President Reagan is demanding that Israel give back strategic land that they critically need. This could, unquestionably open the door for the Soviet Union at a time when they are hungry and they see the United States is not officially standing by Israel.

I believe if America stood up and boldly made a strategic commitment to the State of Israel, recognizing Jerusalem as its capitol, that not only would it stop the Soviet Union in its tracks but put a stop to the enormous amount of Arab blackmail and terrorism—which is absolutely destroying South and Central America.

YES, '83 will be the most critical year in the history of the United States of America. A nation will make a decision to either stand with Israel or to pull away from her. All indications are that without the body of Christ rising up in intercessory prayer, challenging the powers of hell, that the handwriting is on the wall. But I believe God's people will accept the challenge and turn this nation back, giving birth to one of the greatest revivals that has ever hit the United States and the State of Israel . . . because of our obedience to the Word of God.

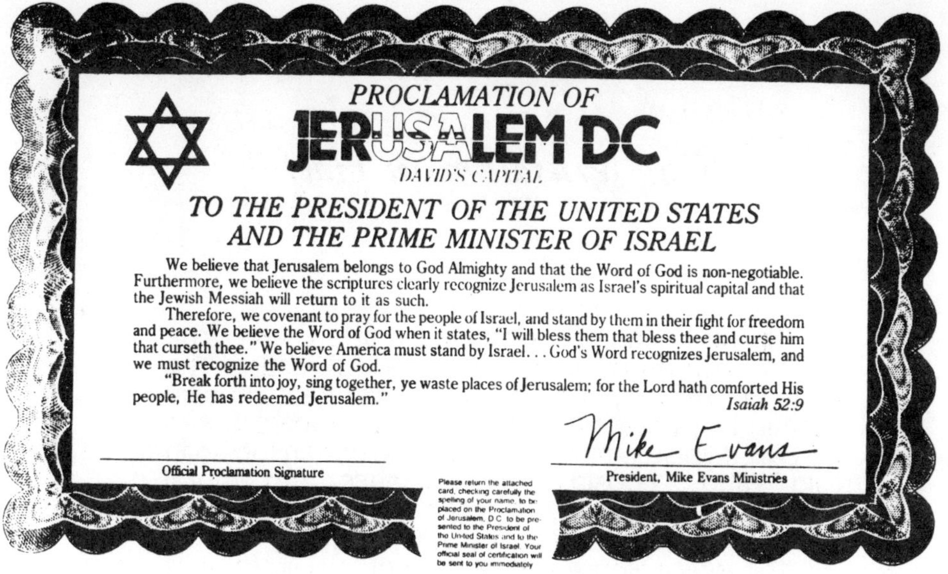

PROCLAMATION OF

JERUSALEM DC

DAVID'S CAPITAL

TO THE PRESIDENT OF THE UNITED STATES AND THE PRIME MINISTER OF ISRAEL

We believe that Jerusalem belongs to God Almighty and that the Word of God is non-negotiable. Furthermore, we believe the scriptures clearly recognize Jerusalem as Israel's spiritual capital and that the Jewish Messiah will return to it as such.

Therefore, we covenant to pray for the people of Israel, and stand by them in their fight for freedom and peace. We believe the Word of God when it states, "I will bless them that bless thee and curse him that curseth thee." We believe America must stand by Israel. . . God's Word recognizes Jerusalem, and we must recognize the Word of God.

"Break forth into joy, sing together, ye waste places of Jerusalem; for the Lord hath comforted His people, He has redeemed Jerusalem."
Isaiah 52:9

Official Proclamation Signature

Mike Evans
President, Mike Evans Ministries

Please return the attached card, checking carefully the spelling of your name, to be placed on the Proclamation of Jerusalem, D.C. to be presented to the President of the United States and to the Prime Minister of Israel. Your official seal of certification will be sent to you immediately

Bear Season

The Bear is moving closer and closer toward Jerusalem. Recently, Afghan guerrillas killed more than 160 Russian soldiers in a hit and run attack in northern Afghanistan . . . Richard Armitage, Assistant Secretary of Defense for International Security Affairs, said, "The Soviet Union has 750 medium-and short-range missiles in the Far East, including 135 SS-20 rocket launchers." He said that Soviet ground forces have increased from 150,000 in 1965 to almost one-half million in the Middle East.

The Soviet Union has made an official decision that if America endeavors to participate in any future Middle East wars, either directly or indirectly, the Soviet Union would immediately airlift significant Russian divisions into the Middle East, basing these divisions in Syria.

Recently, Soviet-built TU-22 warplanes bombed a section of the southeast Sudanese capital. □

"Cut Jerusalem In Half!"

This heartbreaking declaration was the consensus of the Secretary of State, The National Security Council and President Ronald Reagan in a meeting with the Saudi Ambassador, a Foreign Minister and King Fahd. President Reagan told Fahd, "considerable influence and moral persuasion must be used by Saudi Arabia to bring about direct negotiations between Israel."

The White House released an official statement saying, "We are trying to foster modern Arab support for Jordan's King Hussein and his participation in direct talks with Israel. We are optimistic over renewed discussions between Hussein and PLO Leader, Yasir Arafat, and that lasting peace will come when Israel returns the land it captured in the '67 War."

During a meeting at Mr. Evans home recently a high-level Israeli official informed Mr. Evans that the PLO in Jordan is planning to establish a Moslem Capital, which will take in one-half of Jerusalem and a large percentage of Israel's strategic land.

He mentioned that the majority of the world is behind cutting Jerusalem in half — which would definitely change everything. Jerusalem would no longer be called Jerusalem, the Holy City, but Jerusalem, the City of Armageddon.

President Ronald Reagan and King Fahd of Saudi Arabia at State Department Ceremony.

That same Israeli official asked, "Why is America, a Christian nation, trying to cut our Holy City in two?" He said, "Prophecies of the Bible said we would come back to this land and that Jerusalem would be ours again. God Almighty told King David it would be our capital. Six million of our people have already died in the Holocaust. Another three million are being persecuted in the Soviet Union. Most of these Arab countries, including Jordan, are buying arms from the Soviets and are working with the Soviets in many ways. Shall we give this land to the Soviet Union? If Saudi Arabia thinks the solution to peace is solving the Palestinian problem, then why don't they do so? They have the land (more than a hundred times the size of our country). They can give the Palestinians some land. And if they only gave a nickel for every dollar that they've made from U.S. oil sales, the Palestinians would have enough to provide a better standard of living than most Americans have."

A Letter to the President

Dear President Reagan,

Thank you so much for your most recent card and for the gracious time you afforded me in the White House.

Mr. President, I would remind you of a short sentence taken from my lengthy message, which was read to the 97th Session of the Congress of the United States, on why America must stand by Israel.

"We believe one of the reasons America has been blessed over the years is because we have stood with Israel. This promise is taken from Genesis 12:3, 'I will bless them that bless thee.' For Biblical reasons first and foremost, we support the state of Israel."

Mr. President, I consider it a great honor and privilege to stand by you, pray for you, and serve on many distinguished committees encouraging evangelicals to support the positions that you support, such as your opposition to abortion, your strong position in favor of prayer in schools, etc. But I would remind you of the words that you told us — "Do not support me — support the positions that I take — and only support them if they are right."

Mr. President, when it comes to Jerusalem, it is not important what I say, or what the beloved evangelical friends who will be lending their names to this letter say. But what is important to us is what God Almighty says. His Holy Word acknowledges Jerusalem as Israel's capital.

We appeal to you for the sake of everything that our great nation stands for — to not divide this Holy City and give half of Jerusalem and much of Israel's territories to the PLO and Jordan.

At the last meeting in the White House when you invited over 90 distinguished evangelical leaders to meet with your top advisors on the Middle East, I stood publicly and challenged your National Security Advisor, Robert McFarland, and I quote:

"Mr. McFarland, you said that our President states the status of Jerusalem must be determined by negotiations. Mr. McFarland, with whom will the President negotiate? God Almighty has already determined the status of Jerusalem. We, as evangelical Christians, consider the Word of God to be non-negotiable! For the sake of this great nation, please do not endeavor to frustrate God's prophetic plan."

Mr. President, I appeal to you to consider these sentiments that I expressed to your National Security Advisor. We also appeal to you to not encourage Jordan to negotiate over Jerusalem. Jordan has Soviet advisors in its country, and is purchasing Soviet missiles as you well know.

Israel is faced with the greatest economic crisis in the history of her nation – mainly due to the escalation of arms sales in the Middle East. We would humbly appeal to you to please consider the fact that we do want a portion of our tax dollars used for the economic assistance of Israel.

In that spirit, we would also appeal to you, Mr. President, to use your great office and power to resolve this horrible tragedy in behalf of twelve-thousand Ethiopian Jews. They are dying daily in the Sudan because the airlifts were thwarted when news was leaked by the U.S. press.

In the same spirit, we humbly appeal to you to encourage the CIA's release of records on Joseph Mengele to the proper individuals so he can be apprehended.

Mr. President, I express my deepest support and prayers for you, for your health, and for God's richest blessings upon your family.

The reason I'm asking many of my partners and friends to lend their support to this letter is because I know many of your advisors are being influenced by "liberal Christians" that the evangelicals really do not care about Israel. But, Mr. President, that is not so.

These precious people who are lending their support to this letter, join me in respectfully and graciously pleading with you to consider the fact that your second term was a prophetic mandate from Bible-believing Christians to, above all, stand on the Word of God and honor the God of the Word.

If you'll do this, He will truly honor you.

Sincerely in prayer
Mike Evans
Evangelist Mike Evans

What Evangelical Leaders are saying about Israel and Bible Prophecy.

"Pray for the peace of Jerusalem: they shall prosper that love thee." *Psalm 122:6*

"Right at the very top of our priorities must be an unswerving commitment and devotion to the State of Israel, to the survival of that only free democracy in the Middle East, and a commitment to pray for the peace of Jerusalem. I firmly believe that a part of the Christian faith is praying for and supporting the peace of Israel. I spend a great deal of my time on this subject. I know it's unpopular and I get a lot of 'heat' because of it. But Mike Evans is to be commended and many others who are taking a stand for support for the State of Israel."

JERRY FALWELL

"I think that the history of the Christian world is inextricably linked up with the history and destiny of Israel. And, without question, when God favors Zion, He will also be favoring His people all around the world. And that's why we should pray for the peace of Jerusalem and the blessing of God upon Jerusalem. The future of this Nation may be at stake, because God will bless those that bless Israel. And God will curse those that curse Israel."

PAT ROBERTSON

"What a fulfillment of prophecy! What a testimony of faith in God! What a future Israel has! And what a contribution Israel has made, is making and will make! All of us of the Christian faith here in America salute you, we send you our warmest love and greetings. You're constantly in our prayers. . .and we, too, say ' "Oh ! Jerusalem Oh ! Jerusalem." ' And we send our love and our prayers."

ORAL ROBERTS

"First of all, I want to say, God Bless You, Mike Evans for what you're doing in bringing the world's attention to the vital, super importance of the Nation of Israel and Jerusalem. The Jewish people, the most mistreated people in all of the world, need to know right now that there is a strong Bible, God-centered remnant of people in the Christian world, that because of our heritage in Jesus, we pray, with all of our hearts, for the peace of Jerusalem."

KENNETH COPELAND

"You can not read and take literally the prophecies of the Bible and come away thinking God in any way has forsaken His purpose with the Jew. He has sworn He will bring them back in the last days. Genesis, Chapter 12, when God created the State of Israel out of one man Abraham. He made a promise to Abraham and to all of his descendents. He said, 'I will bless those who bless you; and I will curse those who curse you.' History shows that every nation that has turned against Israel and the Jewish people, and has mistreated them, has very soon disappeared as a power."

HAL LINDSEY

"I was in Washington the other day. I had the opportunity and privilege of addressing some of the most powerful Jewish rabbis in the nation. Scores of them gathered in the executive office building close to the White House there in Washington. I was asked to say a few words. I made this statement. . .I told the people we were very happy, as the rabbis listened, to be in Washington D.C., the center of democracy for the whole world. But soon, and not so very long, men seeking peace and men carrying out the affairs of high government, would gather in Jerusalem D.C. There was a hush that filled the room. Washington D.C. they could understand. . .But Jerusalem D.C. they didn't understand. And then I closed it with these two words. . . Jerusalem D.C., David's Capital. Tears

filled eyes . . . Men's faces paled. . . Rabbis bowed their heads and some lifted their eyes. They caught the import of it. And that is it. . . Jerusalem D.C., David's Capital. America must make that decision, because that's the Bible. . . and that's fact! America must take a stand. America must take a position, and that position must be in favor of God and the Bible as I've said, and I say it again for impact, 'the future of this nation may be at stake, because God will bless those that bless Israel, and God will curse them that curse Israel.' "

JIMMY SWAGGART

"We're seeing fulfilled the prophecies of the Old Testament, daily, in all of the things that have taken place in Israel."

REX HUMBARD

"The Bible says we're to pray for the peace of Jerusalem. It also figures if we're going to pray for it we need to work for it, and contribute toward the peace of Jerusalem. The best part is, the peace of Jerusalem also helps guarantee the peace of the Middle East."

PAT BOONE

Appendix D

The Premillennial Scenario According To Chick Comics

Chick Publications (Chino, Calif.) is a fundamentalist Christian Ministry that distributes literature, primarily in the format of small comic books, for evangelistic purposes. The following panels from the booklet titled *SUPPORT YOUR LOCAL JEW,* Chick Publications, P.O. Box 662, Chino, Calif. 91710. (714-987-0771)

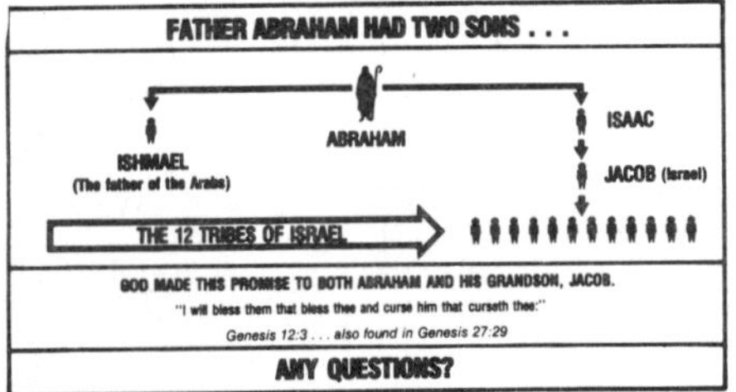

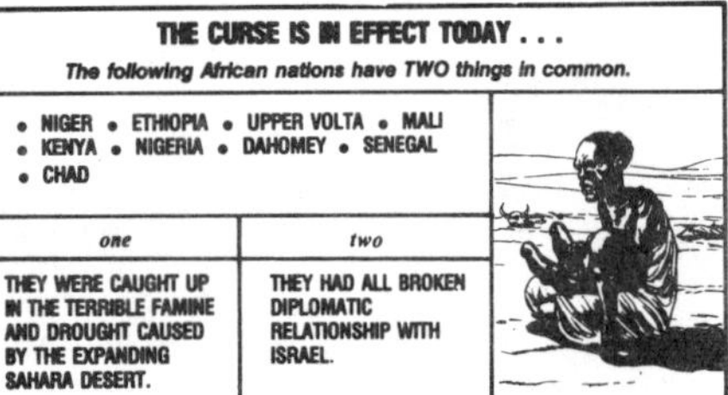

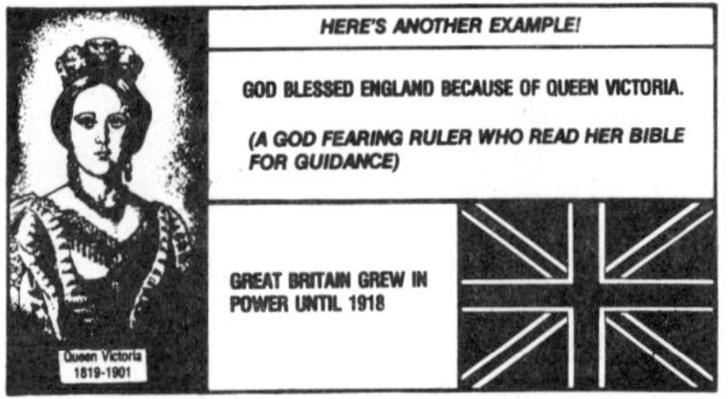

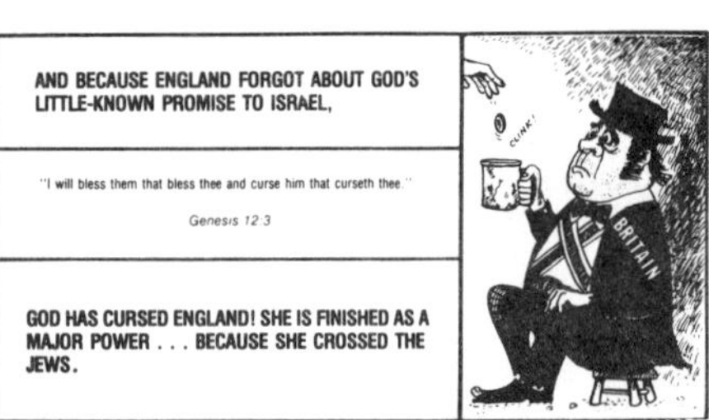

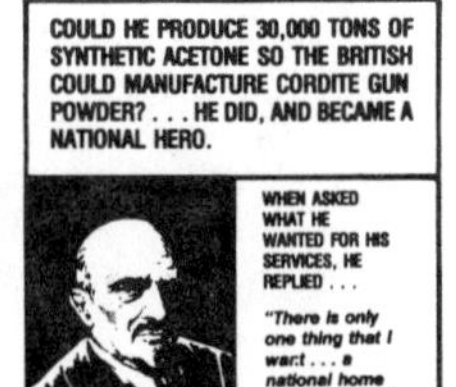

THE BALFOUR DECLARATION ISSUED IN NOV. 1917 WAS BRITAIN'S PROMISE TO THE JEWS OF A HOMELAND IN PALESTINE.

PALESTINE, FORMERLY BELONGING TO TURKEY, WAS NOW PLACED UNDER BRITISH CONTROL IN 1923.

HERE'S WHERE THE TROUBLE STARTED!

*TO FAVOR THE ARABS, BRITISH POLITICIANS *DIVIDED PALESTINE GIVING THE ARABS THE BEST LAND. JEWISH IMMIGRATION WAS CUT TO A TRICKLE AND EVENTUALLY STOPPED.*

* Fall & Rise of Israel by Hull — Zondervan Pub., Pg 137

IN 1938, AS HITLER'S BLOOD BATH STARTED, JEWS PLEADED AND BEGGED FOR PERMISSION TO ENTER PALESTINE.

THEIR CRIES FELL ON DEAF EARS . . . *BRITISH POLICY WOULD NOT BE CHANGED! . . . AND THESE JEWS WERE PUT INTO NAZI OVENS.

* "The Fall & Rise of Israel," by Hull/ Zondervan Publ., Pgs. 198-200

ON MAY 14, 1948, THE U.N. VOTED FOR ISRAEL TO BECOME A NATION!

BRITISH REACTION

- THE BRITISH OPPOSED THE JEWISH STATE
- THE BRITISH BACKED THE ARABS
- THE CRACK TRANSJORDAN ARAB LEGION WAS STAFFED WITH BRITISH OFFICERS
- THE BRITISH DISARMED THE JEWS.

The Bible says . . . "I will bless them that bless thee and curse him that curseth thee:" *Genesis 12:3*

ENGLAND, TODAY, IS A NATION IN DEEP TROUBLE!

RUSSIA HAS LONG BEEN THE ENEMY OF ISRAEL

OVER 2500 YEARS AGO THE PROPHET EZEKIEL, PREDICTED THE TERRIBLE *DESTRUCTION OF RUSSIA WHEN SHE MOVES AGAINST ISRAEL.

THAT ACTION SETS OFF WORLD WAR III, A ONE DAY FIRE WAR —** AS A RESULT ¼ OF THE WORLD'S POPULATION DIES.

*38th chapter of Ezekiel (Magog ancient name for Russia)
**Rev 6:8

INTERESTING NOTE: — ISRAEL SURVIVES THIS WAR!

RUSSIA WILL ATTACK THE U.S. WHEN SHE MOVES ON ISRAEL

HOW BADLY THE U.S. WILL BE HIT DEPENDS ON HOW LOYAL WE ARE TO ISRAEL.

IT ALL DEPENDS ON OIL!

OUR SENATORS AND CONGRESSMEN WHO VOTED AGAINST DEVELOPING ENERGY RESOURCES HAVE PLACED US IN A PRECARIOUS SITUATION.

NOW WE ARE HEAVILY DEPENDENT ON ARAB OIL.

Just back from a trip through the Mideast, an emissary from the treasury brought this message . . .
*"Every Arab leader I talked to says that if there is another war in the area we'll see an oil embargo that will make the 1973-74 version look like child's play."

*U.S. News & World Report April 26, 1976 pg. 9

WILL WE DUMP ISRAEL FOR A TANK OF GAS? . . . IF WE DO, GOD HELP US . . . (AND YOU KNOW HE WON'T!)

ARE WE BLESSING ISRAEL WHEN WE ARM HER ENEMIES?

After World War III, Israel enters "The time of Jacob's trouble" . . . the worst 7 years of her existence *⅔ of all Jews die.

* "And it shall come to pass, that in all the land, saith the Lord, two parts therein shall be cut off and die; but the third shall be left therein." *Zech. 13:8*

At the close of that 7 year period, the armies of the world move to destroy Israel at the Battle of Armaggedon . . .

When all is lost . . . her Messiah bursts through the clouds and saves her.

He destroys the invading armies. Then He takes over all the governments . . . no more wars! He is the Prince of Peace.

Israel gets her greatest shock . . . her Messiah will have *nail prints in His hands.

Israel's Messiah is known in the New Testament as the Lord Jesus Christ. All this will occur at his 2nd coming.

**Psalms 22:16-Zech. 12:10*

In the Old Testament God wanted Israel to be a light to the world . . . a Holy nation of people representing Him.

THEY FAILED MISERABLY!

The evil that has come upon Israel was depicted in the Old Testament . . . God warned them not to sin or they would pay the consequences.

For a frightening revelation, read Leviticus, chapter 26 . . . but before you look down your nose . . . remember, every other nation has done the same thing.

The nations will give an account before God, just like every man or woman who ever lived . . . both Jew and *Gentile.

**A non-Jew*

I WILL GIVE AN ACCOUNT FOR *EVERY-THING* I'VE EVER DONE?

The Bible says . . . And as it is appointed unto men once to die, but after this the judgment. *Hebrews 9:27*

(GULP) I'M NOT READY FOR JUDGMENT! IF GOD LOVED ME, HE'D MAKE A WAY FOR ME TO GET OUT OF THIS MESS!

HE DID!

Appendix E

RELIGION

Arguing Armageddon

For the first time in American history, the end of the world has become a campaign issue. It arose during the second presidential debate, when Ronald Reagan was asked if he truly believes that the world is headed for a "nuclear Armageddon." Reagan acknowledged "philosophical discussions" about the coincidence between current events and Biblical signs portending the last days, but the commander in chief insisted that he has never said that "we must plan according to Armageddon." Reagan's answer, however, did not close the case. Last week a coalition of 100 Christian and Jewish leaders warned that the president may be unduly influenced in foreign affairs by a "theology of nuclear Armageddon" that, they charged, is being propagated by fundamentalist preachers to sanction the administration's hard line on nuclear defense. The critics' Washington press conference was loudly interrupted by leaders of the New Religious Right, who countercharged that the mainline coalition was simply playing secular politics.

For most American voters, the debate over Armageddon may be a trifle arcane. In simplest terms, Reagan's clerical critics suspect that the president really believes—as he has said—that the Soviet Union is an "evil empire" and that the United States is therefore fighting God's own enemies. Further, they fear the president has adopted the hard-core fundamentalist view that the Biblical battle of Armageddon is at hand, making any search for peace futile since God himself plans a nuclear holocaust. But the Rev. Jerry Falwell, among other Reagan defenders, insists that the critics misunderstand both the Bible and the fundamentalists. "I do not believe that there will be a nuclear war," he says.

Pulp: On the other hand, Reagan is known to have read and discussed with fundamentalist friends like Falwell and singer Pat Boone such pulp versions of Biblical prophecies as Hal Lindsey's best-selling "The Late Great Planet Earth," which strongly hints of a nuclear Armageddon. On at least one occasion, in 1980, he mused on television that "we may be the generation that sees Armageddon." As for Falwell, he did say in a 1981 interview with the Los Angeles Times that Armageddon is "at that time when I believe that there will be some nuclear holocaust on this earth . . . It could be 50 years. [But] I don't think we have that long."

Prophesying the end of the world is a staple of fundamentalism, of course; so is retooling of the Biblical details to fit evangelistic need. In a standard scenario, the end begins with the "Rapture"—a word fundamentalists use to describe the rescue of all true Christians to a place with Jesus somewhere "in the air." This is followed by seven years of "Tribulation" for those left behind. Then a league headed by Russia will threaten war on Israel. Israel will join forces with the apparently benevolent leader of a 10-nation consortium (the European Common Market?). From the east will come a huge army of Chinese and Indians. God will then destroy the Soviet Union, killing—in Falwell's interpretation—"83 percent" of the Soviet soldiers.

Antichrist: But the benevolent European will turn out to be the Antichrist, who will enter the restored Temple in Jerusalem and demand veneration. Israel will resist. Next, Christ will return with an army of raptured saints to defeat the Antichrist at the Battle of Armageddon, north of Jerusalem. Many Jews will then accept Jesus as their savior and a thousand years of peace will ensue until the Last Judgment.

JOHN FICARA—Newsweek

Reagan with Boone and broadcasters: What does he believe?

This detailed doctrine is not accepted by most Christians. But it exerts a strong hold on those brought up on it: evangelical church historian Tim Weber of Denver Seminary recalls that as a child he once lost track of his mother in a store and thought she had been raptured. "There was never anything political about the doctrine then," says Weber. "Up to the 1970s it was mainly an evangelistic tool for winning souls: it promised converts would avoid the slaughter of Armageddon by being raptured."

Political Twist: Indeed, no scriptural passage or symbol provides the basis for imagining an American role at Armageddon, which rules out any idea that a U.S.-Soviet nuclear confrontation would somehow fulfill a prophecy. Most fundamentalists recognize this. Even so, some of Reagan's supporters have given Biblical apocalypticism a contemporary political twist. Author Lindsey—who claims he has lectured at the Pentagon—urges in a more recent book, "The 1980s: Countdown to Armageddon," that the United States maintain an aggressive nuclear stance. So does Falwell. Since God himself will destroy his enemies at Armageddon, they seem to say, no one need fear that a superpower will beat him to the ultimate punch. But a strong national defense ensures a safe America for Christians until the moment they are raptured out of danger.

How much of all this Ronald Reagan believes is known only to him. In the past he seems to have accepted the fundamentalists' apocalyptic language as at least a metaphor for mankind's most dangerous dilemma. But last week even Jerry Falwell was calling on the candidates of both parties to "repudiate . . . any extremist world view which demands a nuclear Armageddon."

KENNETH L. WOODWARD

GIRAUDON—ART RESOURCE

Jean Cousin the Younger's 'Last Judgment': A nuclear holy war?

NEWSWEEK/NOVEMBER 5, 1984

Appendix F

Slouching towards Armageddon: Links with Evangelicals

By LOUIS RAPOPORT

INDIFFERENCE saved the day. Most Israelis are simply apathetic about the Temple Mount, the site of the First and Second Temples, of the rectangular rock upon which Abraham was to sacrifice Isaac at God's command. And this apathy is what prevented the Jewish terrorist underground from carrying out its central mission: to blow up the golden Dome of the Rock, the Moslem shrine built around that piece of granite which, in Jewish lore, is the foundation-stone of the universe.

The plan was to hasten the advent of the Messiah and of Redemption, by setting off the war between Gog and Magog, the last *jihad*, and ushering in the End of Days. But the co-organizer of the terrorist underground found that he and his comrades were too far ahead of the people, the timing was not quite right, there would be a comprehension gap among the mothers whose sons would be slaughtered in the ensuing holy war.

The messianic Jews share a similar spirit with the religious extremists of all nations. Religious intoxication is sweeping the world, including America with its tens of millions of fundamentalist Christians.

In this climate, a group of minor actors has been moving about the stage attempting to forge strong links between some Christian Evangelicals and the zealots of Jewish religious nationalism, trying to raise the collective conscience, to educate the people so that they'll *care*. There is a definite comic-opera flavour to the whole story, despite the serious issues that are raised.

Enter Stanley Goldfoot, a former South African who was once an "intelligence" man in the Stern group underground – he was among those jailed by the young State of Israel in connection with the murder of UN envoy Count Bernadotte in 1948. In the early 1970s, he was the publisher of a right-wing journal called *The Times of Israel*, and was one of the founders of the Faithful of the Temple Mount, a rather lame little group that makes periodic and peaceful attempts to pray on the Temple Mount. (The Mount is administered by the Moslem wakf, or trust, and neither Jews nor Christians are allowed to pray there.)

But there was a parting of the ways with the Faithful a couple of years ago. "I'm afraid they've lost their way," says the greying, courtly Goldfoot, who possesses the mellifluous voice of a hammy Shakespearean actor. There is something markedly histrionic about him.

Soon after the split with the Faithful, Goldfoot set up the Jerusalem Temple Foundation, whose board consists of himself and five U.S. Evangelicals.

Goldfoot sloughs off charges by some members of the Faithful that he has become the main instrument for fundamentalist Christians attempting to convert Jews. He is close-mouthed about a $50,000 gift

Jerusalem Post International Edition, June 17-24, 1984

from one of his board members (Oklahoma oil and land wheeler-dealer Terry Risenhoover), which members of the Faithful felt should not be dispensed exclusively by Goldfoot.

When I first interviewed Goldfoot some months ago, he denied that there ever was a $50,000 donation. Then, with a guffaw shared with his wife, he said, "That $50,000 was given expressly to establish the headquarters of the Jerusalem Temple Foundation...Private people came up with the money – for a library, reading room, offices – but I decided it's not the right time. Too much of a headache." The atmosphere was wrong: His wife said that Jewish anti-missionary activists might blow up the headquarters.

Now, that $50,000 – or a very similar $50,000 – has cropped up in a major article published last week in *The New Republic*, which states that Goldfoot is the main conduit for funds from American fundamentalists to nationlist fundamentalists in Israel, including money for the defence of the "Lifta group" of messianists who tried to blow up the Dome of the Rock a few months before the Gush Emunim terrorists were rounded up.

The article in *The New Republic*, by Michael and Barbara Ledeen (he is a former aide to Alexander Haig and a frequent contributor to *Commentary*), makes the Goldfoot operation seem big-time indeed. But it isn't. The press hankers for sensational revelations, and it was no suprise that an Israeli newspaper, *Hadashot*, splashed the story on its front page and claimed – totally inaccurately – that "millions of dollars" were being funnelled from the Evangelicals to Israeli Temple Mount fanatics. Goldfoot says that Michael Ledeen is a "good friend" of his. He adds, in a stage whisper, that "all you journalists are liars." But one senses that he is not at all displeased by the publicity.

The article in *The New Republic*, and the much exaggerated *Hadashot* translation, drew fire last week from Texas Evangelical minister Dr. Hilton Sutton, of Mission to America (and also a board member of the Jerusalem Temple Foundation). Sutton threatened to sue both publications for saying that Mission to America has contributed large sums to the Jewish terrorist underground.

According to all available evidence, the terrorists needed little money to finance their operations. And it is highly unlikely that they would have sought any outside funds whatsoever. Sutton, ignoring Michael Ledeen's staunchly conservative background, said it was all part of a "left-wing" plot against avid supporters of Israel.

But where did the money funnelled to Stanley Goldfoot end up? When asked if he is willing to give a public accounting, Goldfoot responded, "Of course not." One can only speculate on what he told Ledeen, and why.

THERE ARE significant, and to some minds, worrisome, links between a handful of American Evangelical leaders and right-wing Israelis like Goldfoot. Some of the personalities on his board are important men. One of them, physicist Lambert Dolphin, heads a key section of the world's most massive research conglomerate, the Stanford Research Institute, a $200-million-a-year concern whose main clients are the U.S. government and corporations like Bechtel. Board member Terry Risenhoover is received at the Reagan White House, and chaired this year's "national prayer breakfast in honour of Israel." Jerry Falwell, upon whom Menachem Begin bestowed the Jabotinsky Medal, is sympathetic. But there is something overblown about the whole story, a sense of agitprop accepted as reality. Goldfoot's organization apparently has no general membership at all. When pressed, Goldfoot says he has "30-40 million" supporters.

There's a family crest above the door of Goldfoot's spacious Jerusalem penthouse. When asked what it represents, Goldfoot, who describes himself as an "entrepreneur," answers resonantly, "I made it up."

Before the Temple Mount plotters – both the Lifta terrorists and the Gush Emunim terror group – were arrested, Goldfoot and Dolphin planned to hover one day just before dawn in a helicopter 300 metres above the Temple Mount and the Holy of Holies (where the Ark of the Covenant was kept), and to X-ray and probe the innards of the mount with Dolphin's induced polarization set, Cesium Beam Magnetometer, downhole Borescope television and high-power Dipole-Dipole Resistivity Set to find out just what is buried down there.

Dolphin comes to Israel frequently, and has used his sophisticated gear at Herodion and Hebron. But his real interest, and that of his fellow Evangelical and fundamentalist preachers and laymen, is the Temple Mount – they believe that Jesus cannot come again until the Temple Mount is restored to the Jews and the Temple is rebuilt (and then destroyed for the third time). "It was in the Second Temple that Jesus worshipped, taught, and threw out the money changers on two occasions. It was in the Temple Court that the Christian Church was born," reads an official Stanford Research Institute International brochure put out by Dolphin.

Goldfoot frequently speaks to groups of Evangelicals touring Israel about the importance of the Mount, and has toured America on the Evangelical circuit. When he spoke before Reverend Chuck Smith's Calvary Chapel in Costa Mesa, California, a few months ago, the church's lavish 3,000-seat auditorium was filled to overflowing. The reverend sent a Cadillac equipped with a bar and a telephone to pick Goldfoot up at the airport, and it was champagne treatment all the way.

Goldfoot says he plays the tape of his speech every night before going to bed, "just to hear the applause." They loved him there in Costa Mesa, as he recited Jewish prayers that implore the Almighty to "Build Thy Temple speedily." To the wild applause of the believers, he said: "Jerusalem is not truly liberated yet – its heart is still under alien control. There is no freedom of worship on the Temple Mount, not for the Jews and not for the Christians...the wakf employs thugs who will prevent you from praying there." He does not add that if the Orthodox establishment ever came to administer the Mount, his Christian friends would probably still be barred from praying there.

GOLDFOOT PLAYS a loose game with history. In describing Christian holy spots on the Mount in an interview, he mentions the spot where

Jesus' brother, St. James, was martyred – "stabbed or stoned to death." Who killed James? "Why, Moslems, of course," says Goldfoot. He catches his error – we have to wait another 600 years or so for Mohammed and his followers to appear – and says, "Well, not Moslems of course. The people at the time...[lowering his voice:] between you and me and the lamppost, it was the Jews that killed him."

Perhaps flippancy is the wrong tone here. But a certain amount is unavoidable – for instance, tycoon Terry Risenhoover, who chaired the prayer breakfast in which all the major American Jewish organizations took part and which was addressed by Ambassador Meir Rosenne, is under investigation by the FBI, according to Goldfoot, in an alleged land fraud case.

And now it turns out that Risenhoover may not even be Risenhoover – he went up to the Temple Mount with Goldfoot one day, and said, "I am Nehemiah..." Which raised even Goldfoot's eyebrows. (Nehemiah, or Zerubbabel, was the restorer of the Temple in ancient times, and is to be the Messiah's Herald one great day, according to Jewish legend.)

It's difficult to ascertain just how much money Risenhoover has given Goldfoot – one reliable Christian source told me that the sum far exceeds $50,000, and that only poison fruit has grown from its seeding. When an American-Jewish colleague of mine called Risenhoover to ask him about the money and related questions, he was told, "Repent, and make aliya." In answer to a letter I sent Risenhoover, I received a 17-page typed response written by Risenhoover, who serves as chairman of the Jerusalem Temple Foundation, and Douglas W. Krieger, its executive director. My query about money elicited the line: "We have not given enough – that is how much we have given." This was followed by quotations from the prophet Malachi, such as "Will a man rob God? Yet you are robbing me!..."

Risenhoover, 37, describes himself as a "classical Southern Baptist" whose ventures include drilling for oil in Israel. He and Krieger and their colleagues believe they have been stirred up by God to prepare for the Messiah's (second) coming. They quote Revelation Chapter 11, saying that a final spiritual battle will take place over the Temple site and that Israel and the Church will together triumph. The evil King of the North has transformed himself into the USSR in their eyes. A major war is coming, one that will also involve Egypt; and Damascus may be destroyed. Israel on the millennial maps of the Evangelicals includes great chunks of Egypt, Lebanon and Syria.

Along with Lambert Dolphin, they condemned the abortive attempt (by the Lifta group) to blow up the Dome of the Rock. But they feel that "violence" is being done to the most sacred site "when Jewish prayer books are seized by Temple Guards from devout Jewish women..."

They say they don't believe that all Jews have to convert to Christianity, but that a Christian isn't worth his salt unless he "bears witness" and at least tries to woo the Jews.

SOME OF THE biggest names in the Evangelical world are connected to the men on the board of the

Jerusalem Temple Foundation – which is still little more than a letterhead organization, but which has been given a big boost by the *New Republic* article, however critical it may have sounded. The president and founder of the Prayer Breakfast for Israel is Ed McAteer, head of the influential, staunchly conservative Roundtable organization and a candidate for senator from Tennessee (Goldfoot stopped off during his American tour to give McAteer's campaign a shot in the arm with his rousing speech about the Temple Mount).

Dr. Charles E. Monroe, another board member and head of a San Diego theology school, met in recent months with the chief rabbis and with the prime minister's adviser on Christian matters, Harry Hurwitz.

Yisrael Medad, a resident of Shiloh who works with Goldfoot and also with El Har Hashem, another minor group campaigning for Jewish rights on the Temple Mount, guided Risenhoover and Dolphin during one of their trips to Israel, introducing them to the "Temple lobby" at the Knesset: Yehuda Perah (Liberals), Geula Cohen (Tehiya) and Rabbi Haim Druckman (Matzad).

Unlike Goldfoot, Medad admits to wanting "political and monetary support from the Christian fundamentalists... We're looking to the Christians for help, not out of any theological identity of views, but because we haven't gotten any support from Jews." Medad, a Tehiya and Gush Emunim activist, said two months before the arrest of the Jewish terrorist underground that the Temple issue had become a new and critical focus of leaders of the "believers' camp," since it combined religious and nationalistic goals.

THE LINK between this small group of individual Evangelicals and Israelis is indicative of a much broader alliance between the reborn Christians and American Jews. The traditional alliance between American Jews and liberal Christians is over, mainly because the liberal churches are seen as anti-Israel, while the conservative Evangelicals and Fundamentalists are down-the-line pro-Israel.

AIPAC, the Israel lobby in Washington, has taken on a full-time Christian liaison, whose main task is to deal with the conservative Christians. Some major Jewish organizations now devote a great deal of attention to the emerging alliance, with hardly a second thought about what it means to jump into bed with the fundamentalist movement.

The Israeli government is no less enthusiastic than the American Jewish organizations, although one official I spoke to was wary of some individual Evangelical leaders. Refering to Terry Risenhoover, for instance, the well-informed source said: "He is making his way rapidly, because he is loaded. But he is way out... as is Goldfoot."

Reverend Jim DeLoach of Houston, Texas, is another of the five Christians on the six-man board of the Jerusalem Temple Foundation. DeLoach seems typical of the second-line leadership that supports Israel unequivocally. He grew up in Alabama, and was anti-Semitic, he says, until he was "reborn" at age 22 and began to see "that the Bible was a Jewish book." He wears a diamond ring that combines the Star of David-with the Cross; on his lapel he pins a double flag – America and Israel. "I'm a Christian Zionist willing to declare myself," he says. "I'm a pro-American and am pro-Israel."

He's not bothered by Orthodox Jewish critics or other opponents of the alliance between the Evangelicals and Israel. "They have legitimate gripes, like against missionizing," he says. But he won't come out squarely against missions to the Jews. Asked about the tens of thousands of dollars given by Evangelicals to Stanley Goldfoot, he says, "We know there was gentile involvement in the financing and building of both the First and Second Temples. So why not the Third?" He sees it as a privilege to invest in "the dream of Judaism," maintaining at the same time that he would never violate the Orthodox Jewish laws concerning the Temple Mount.

DeLoach and his fellow board members issued a prospectus a few months ago which outlined their "contemplated projects," including financial assistance to Yeshiva Ateret Cohanim ("priestly crown") in the Moslem Quarter of Jerusalem's Old City, a couple of hundred metres from the Temple Mount, where the priestly Temple rites are being studied, help in Jewish efforts to "redeem" buildings in the Moslem Quarter of the Old City, and "preparation for the construction of the Third Temple in Jerusalem."

The architect's plans are already complete – 83-year-old Jacob Yehuda of Safad, a recluse who is considered to be a genius by various Temple Mount sects, has spent his whole life researching the construction of the Third Temple. It's all set to go.

The Dome of the Rock, of course, does not necessarily have to be blown up first. Aryeh Kotzer, principal of a school in Rishon Lezion and a former Lehi underground fighter, has published a booklet in which he maintains that the Dome of the Rock is simply to be incorporated as a part of the Third Temple.

SO FAR, not one of the Evangelical dollars has reached Ateret Cohanim, according to yeshiva spokesman Menachem Bar-Shalom. Ateret Cohanim traces its roots to Rav Avraham Yitzhak Hacohen Kook, the first chief rabbi of Palestine, and his son Zvi Yehuda Kook, spiritual leader of Gush Emunim. The senior Kook once said that the *cohanim*, the members of the priestly caste, must prepare themselves for the Redemption, since the Messiah might come and order the Temple to be rebuilt, and no one would be ready. Rav Kook dropped the idea, but it was picked up over 40 years later by Menachem Hacohen Dan, who founded the yeshiva in 1978.

The Ateret Cohanim people believe they are the vanguard of a movement that is about to take off. Their rabbis forbid them from going up to the Temple Mount until there is a rabbinical ruling allowing Jews to pray there (observant Jews are barred from the Mount by the Chief Rabbinate for fear that they may violate the Holy of Holies).

The yeshiva is contemptuous of such groups as the Faithful of the Temple Mount, which are "ineffective and unimportant." The yeshiva conducts seminars, a field school, and an annual convention on the general subject of the Temple and on specifics about such subjects as animal sacrifice.

The students study the works of Rav Kook and his contemporary, the Hafetz Haim, on priestly duties. Rav Kook wrote that God's message concerning the rebuilding of the Temple was at hand. "That great and glorious day is drawing nigh." He called for study of the rituals and rites, so that everyone would be ready for the Day of Glory. And the messianic fervour is palpable among the people at the yeshiva – the No. 2 defendant in the Jewish underground was said to have been "inspired" after attending lectures on the Temple Mount at Ateret Cohanim.

"The Temple is the top of the pyramid of the Jewish people," says the yeshiva's rabbi, Shlomo Aviner, former rabbi of the religious settlement of Keshet in the Golan. But the time to build the Temple hasn't yet come. First, it's important to bring about Jewish revival. His message is not to jump the gun. Terror methods are completely off base. "It's being done by people who think you can jump, to bring Redemption in an hour." He is not concerned one way or the other about the involvement of the Evangelicals. "It depends on us, not America."

THE PRIME MINISTER's adviser on the Evangelicals, Harry Hurwitz, strongly supports the emerging alliance. It's much better for AIPAC to "go up to the Hill [Capitol Hill] with these Christians to lobby for Israel – because the fundamentalists are the most powerful Christian element in America," he says. Hurwitz served at the Israel Embassy in Washington for three years as information officer. During his tour of duty in the U.S., he worked most closely with David Allen Lewis, head of an umbrella group called the National Christian Leadership Conference for Israel. Lewis has strong links with the Christian Embassy in Jerusalem and with Goldfoot.

Hurwitz notes that there was some Democratic opposition to the growing link between the Jews and the Christian fundamentalists, but "not too much." The Evangelical connection is important for Israel along a wide range of issues. Economically, they are crucial to Israel's tourism industry. Hurwitz gives speeches to visitors such as the "Youth Outreach" wing of "God's World" – a group planning to build a Bible Disneyland in Florida.

Why have these traditionally anti-Semitic elements in América turned into philo-Semites, pro-Israel fanatics? "Maybe they think something is happening here," says Hurwitz. He recalls the delight of being guest of honour at the Alabama governor's mansion back in 1981, soon after the Evangelical-Jewish romance began. Governor Fob James gave a big bash to celebrate Israel's 33rd birthday – it was inspired by his wife, a born-again Christian. Hundreds of participants signed an "I Love Israel" proclamation. They served kosher food. A huge Magen David with 33 outsize candles floated in the executive swimming pool...Joy to the Jews.

THE FACT that the Temple Mount was the prime concern of the Jewish underground that was broken in May came as a surprise to even seasoned reporters who have covered the Mount and the various groups or individuals who have tried to alter the status quo by violent means. For the so-called underground is at the heart of Gush Emunim and the settler movement. They are not fringe nuts like American *baal teshuva* (penitent) Allen Goodman, a Rabbi Kahane fan who went on a rampage on the Mount in April 1982 and killed a Moslem guard. Goodman, whose legal costs were paid by the good rabbi, said he had intended to liberate the Mount and become "king of the Jews."

The Lifta sect that tried to blow up the Moslem shrines on the Mount earlier this year also appeared to be very much on the fringe, as did Kach activist Yoel Lerner, who was convicted in October 1982 of planning to blow up the Dome of the Rock. Michael Rohan, a born-again Australian Christian who set the silver-domed al-Aksa mosque ablaze in 1969, was clearly deranged.

But it should not have come as a shock that some mainstream religious nationalists were also possessed by similar devils. Only a few months ago, on the "Night of the Zealots," Rabbi Kahane's former No. 2 man, Rabbi Ariel, was arrested with 28 others – most from the Kiryat Arba yeshiva – for trying to break into the Temple Mount. The judge condemned the attempt, but let them all go – so what if they were trying to set off the third world war? No doubt, there will be continuing justification by the right-wing for holding "idealistic but perhaps misguided" goals, such as liberating the Temple Mount, at whatever price.

It's not only marginal theatrical characters like Stanley Goldfoot who support the goals of the Jewish terrorists, or who assert Jewish rights on the Temple Mount. Last Yom Kippur police tried to prevent former chief rabbi Shlomo Goren from holding prayers in a room below the Mount. But they relented when Chief of Staff Moshe Levy showed up to join Goren in prayer.

Attorney-General Yitzhak Zamir said recently that any disturbance of the delicate balance on the Mount could have catastrophic results. But the addition of Evangelical Christianity to the already poisonous witches' brew is certain to exacerbate the problem. Rabbi Kahane, in his typically heroic manner, says that he "repulsed Christian overtures connected to the Mount." He said, in a telephone interview some months ago, that Jan Willem van der Hoeven, chief spokesman of the Christian Embassy in Jerusalem, had contacted him, "but I repulsed him – he's a missionary. The Christians would love me to bomb the mosque because they believe it would bring Jesus. I don't want Christians."

Van der Hoeven is critical of the Israeli government for saying "don't rock the boat" over the Temple Mount. The Moslems are usurpers, he says. The Mount should be returned to the Jews – "even if it means Armageddon." But the fundamentalist Christian does not condone violence. "I don't think God needs violence or illegality to accomplish his ways," he says – a sentiment Kahane would fulminate against. Van der Hoeven is disturbed by the fact that Israelis don't care about the Temple Mount. He ascribes this to the fact that "Israelis are too goyified."

But how providential is that apathy, that sluggishness that leaves events to take their own course! At a meeting in Jerusalem of the Temple Mount Faithful, a man named Ze'ev reported on his latest efforts to excite MK Rabbi Haim Druckman about the Temple Mount. "He fell asleep as I was talking," said the outraged zealot. "I'm ashamed of Druckman." □

Appendix G

PAT ROBERTSON'S PERSPECTIVE

A special report to members of The 700 Club

February/March 1980

SPECIAL ISSUE:

PROPHETIC INSIGHTS

FOR THE "DECADE OF DESTINY"

The world crisis has been unfolding at breakneck speed. Events once thought impossible now race by us with alarming rapidity. The entire framework of the world's economic, political, and social systems is being shaken. To understand today's events, we must understand the Bible prophecies which control them. In this special issue, I will discuss several key prophecies relevant to these times.

Jesus Christ gave us the key to modern-day events with these words: "And Jerusalem will be trampled underfoot by the Gentiles [pagans, ungodly, the nations] until the times of the Gentiles be fulfilled." (Luke 21:24.) Put another way, Jesus was saying that the termination of Gentile spiritual privilege and the power that results from it would take place when the Jews took control of Jerusalem.

In 568 B.C., King Nebuchadnezzar of Babylon captured Jerusalem. The city was not controlled by a free Jewish entity until the Six Day War in June 1967, which was 2,535 years after Nebuchadnezzar's action.

June 1967, therefore, becomes the prophetic benchmark for the rapid disintegration of Gentile world power. Consider these events after 1967: A humiliating U.S. loss in Vietnam, the first military loss in our history; virulent worldwide inflation; the fall of the dollar as the great world currency; the worldwide oil crisis; Communist advances throughout Africa; upheaval in Iran; panic in world gold markets; lesser-developed countries on the edge of bankruptcy; a Ponzi pyramid in computer-generated Eurocurrencies threatening an international banking collapse; a plague of abortion, homosexuality, occultism, and pornography; widespread family disintegration; genocide in Cambodia; Russian troops and planes in Cuba; the Afghan invasion; impending worldwide depression; potential Middle East War or even World War III.

It is possible that all of the Biblical prophecies pointing to the Anti-Christ and the Roman Empire were fulfilled in history. "Nero Caesar" spells the number of the Anti-Christ, the mystical "666"; the Emperor of Rome began to believe that he was a god; both the Church and Israel suffered under Rome; and the Roman Empire ultimately fell at the feet of the Christian church.

If this is true, then the battle foretold by Ezekiel could be the last gasp of human revolt against God. Many Orthodox rabbis in Israel now believe that the impending Russian invasion will signal the return of Messiah to Israel.

Nevertheless, I concur with other Bible scholars who feel that the events in modern Europe have great prophetic significance, setting the stage for the reign of Anti-Christ, and one final battle, Armageddon.

If we are reading the Book of Revelation correctly, then this is a possible scenario: Russia will attack Israel to gain unrestricted access to Middle East oil plus a land bridge to the mineral wealth of Africa. The ensuing conflict will undoubtedly cause chaos and disruption, especially to world oil supplies.

The industrial capacity of Europe may be left intact but her economy will be in shambles. The ensuing suffering, rioting, and looting will demand a powerful charismatic leader with dictatorial powers to mobilize the resources of these nations. Virtually overnight, a figure more malevolent than Adolph Hitler could be in complete control of 10 powerful nations.

The next seven years -- possibly coinciding with the Tabernacle period -- will prove a nightmare. It is referred to as the "Great Tribulation." Successive natural disasters, coupled with unbridled demoniac activity, coupled with Satanic dictatorship, coupled with recovery from war and worldwide depression, will create both terror and fantasy. Men will curse God because of their problems and will deify Satan's representative, the Anti-Christ.

At the end of seven years, when he moves by military force to establish his throne in the spiritual capital of the world -- Jerusalem -- Anti-Christ will be destroyed by the return of Jesus Christ. Then Christ will lift His saints both dead and living to be with Him (the "Rapture") and He will lift Israel to a pre-eminent role among the nations of the earth.

* * *

Concluding thoughts: If any of these projections are at all correct, we are entering the most perilous and yet hopeful decade of man's history. Remember that through all this the world will stand. Men will buy and sell, plant and build, marry and give in marriage. Times will be terribly hard, but we will survive. As Jesus put it, "Unless those days had been cut short, no life would have been saved; but for the sake of the elect those days shall be cut short." (Matt. 24:22.)

If the approximate dating of events is even close and if Anti-Christ is yet to come, then we must conclude that there is a man alive today, approximately 27 years old, who is now being groomed to be the Satanic messiah.

We also must conclude that Christians are now in the middle of a brief period of grace when conditions are at an absolutely optimum point for world evangelism. This can be our finest hour!

Under no circumstances do these times give cause to a Christian to fear. Jesus said, "When these things begin to take place, straighten up and lift your heads, because your redemption is drawing near." (Luke 21:28.) Know He is at the very door...Even so, come, Lord Jesus!

Pat Robertson

(EXCERPTED FROM FEB/MAR 1980 NEWSLETTER)

Appendix H

An Hour Before Midnight

JEWISH TOURIST, WHAT CAN YOU DO FOR YOUR PEOPLE AND STATE? FOR YOUSELF!

WHILE IN ISRAEL –

• *Beware of the young Arab who seeks Jewish women.* Often, he tells you he is an Israeli. Ask for his identity card. DO NOT BE ASHAMED (It can save you terrible grief later on). Do not feel pity for him; he is not oppressed. The best thing is not to have anything to do with him. Date only Jews and do not believe for a moment that the Arab who seems so friendly really loves or respects you.

• *If you study at a university in Israel,* be especially wary. Arabs live with Jews in dormitories and they are – to a person – avid followers of the PLO. Do not date them or have social contact with them. Above all, do not enroll in schools such as Hebrew University, Tel Aviv University or Haira University, whose policies towards Arabs are tragic.

• *Do not enroll in or send your child to a kibbutz that is non-religious.* Not only is Judaism lacking but for the most part there is a terrible lack of nationalism and belief in the right of the Jewish people to the entire land. The worst of those who call for a "Palestine" state come from the kibbutzim. And beware of the gentile volunteers who work on almost every non-religious kibbutz. Do not sent your child to Israel through the American Zionist Youth Foundation (AZYF).

• *Do not buy in the market place* of those who do not recognize Israel and who hate the Jewish state. Your money goes to help your enemy.

• *Beware of the Christian missionaries* who cunningly hide behind pro-Israel institutions. Especially be wary of the so-called Christian Embassy and its director William van der Hoeven. This is a clever center of missionary work. Also, beware of book stores along Jaffa Road and other places that are camouflaged missionary centers.

• *Note the anti-religious and anti-nationalist bias of the Jerusalem Post.* Consider very carefully a paper that is so inimical to the best interests of Israel. Do you subscribe to its overseas edition?

• *Vote in the referendum* on whether Israel should be a Jewish State, no matter what, or if it must allow the Arabs to become a majority if their population grows to warrant it. Forms can be gotten at the Kach office, 31 Usishkin Street.

• *Visit the unique, impressive Museum of the Potential Holocaust* for a frightening view of TODAY's Nazis and haters in America. The address is: 31 Usishkin St., Jerusalem.

• *Drop in at a yeshiva for beginners* who seek to return to authentic Judaism. Try Machon Meir on Meiri Boulevard, Jerusalem.

AND BACK IN THE EXILE –

1) *Join the Jewish Defense League* and stand up for people, country and faith.
2) *Continue your Jewish studies.* Keep up the return to real Judaism.
3) *Come on Aliya. Come home, before it is too late.*

THE JEWISH IDEA

Meir Kahane MUST BE HEARD!

At a time of crisis, in this historic moment that holds within it the potential for glorious redemption or terrible tragedy, when Jews seek answers –

The words, thoughts and ideas of the Jewish rebel of the mainstream must be read and listened to, studied and taught, brought to the mind of every Jew in every land –

You can hear Rabbi Kahane speak in Israel
YOUR TEMPLE OR GROUP.

☐ Please send me a list of Rabbi Kahane's writings, and tapes.

☐ I want Rabbi Kahane to speak in my synagogue, group, or home. Please contact me.

Name ______________________

Address ______________________

Phone ______________________

The Jeu'ish Idea ______

P.O.B. 425 Midwood Station
Brooklyn, N.Y. 11230
(212) 934-1223

KACH

ומי כעמך
ישראל
גוי אחד
בארץ

JEWISH DEFENSE LEAGUE OF ISRAEL

31, Usishkin Street, Jerusalem

(02) 690555; 526127; 247202

*"They (Palestinians) Must Go"**

JEW.

IT CAN HAPPEN AGAIN! COME HOME

DEAR AMERICAN JEW!

Two messages that no Jewish leader dares to speak to you about. Your life and those of your people depend on your hearing them:

ONE:

SOME 45 YEARS AGO, the great Zionist leader Z'ev Jabotinsky said: "JEWS! LIQUIDATE THE EXILE BEFORE IT LIQUIDATES YOU!"

SOME 3500 YEARS AGO, the Torah said it first: "AND AMONG THOSE NATIONS SHALL YE FIND NO REST..." (Deuteronomy 28)

TODAY; We of Rabbi Meir Kahane's Kach Movement (JDL of Israel) have created a movement called ZEEERO (Zionist Emergency Exile Evacuation Rescue Organization) to plead with you before it is too late:

"American Jew, Evacuate; flee the graveyard of the exile and escape to Israel, your home, today, before catastrophe strides. A tragedy of massive proportions is coming to America and the spectre of horrible Jew-Hatred looms. Get out. COME HOME. NOW. BEFORE IT IS TOO LATE FOR YOU AND YOUR LOVED ONES.

TWO:

Another message that the little, timid Jewish leaders do not dare to tell you:

Despite all illusions and delusions, the Arabs of Israel are strangers in a Jewish, Zionist State. They hate Israel and look forward to its elimination in favor of a "Palestine." Their incredibly high birth rate threatens Israel as surely as any war. Join with us in calling for a Knesset law and government — JEWS TO ISRAEL, ARABS TO THEIR OWN LANDS.

The removal of the Arabs of Eretz Yisrael will save the Jewish State another Northern Ireland.

American Jew! You are cursed with small, ignorant and myopic Jewish leaders. They will destroy you. Listen to our words. Take heed. It is your life that is at stake.

IT IS TIME

ZEEERO!

(Zionist Emergency Exile Evacuation Rescue Organization)

P.O.B. 425 Midwood Station
Brooklyn, N.Y. 11230
(212) 934-1223

THE ARABS OF ISRAEL: Time Bomb Waiting to Explode

THE KACH MOVEMENT (Jewish Defense League of Israel)
31 Usishkin Street, Jerusalem (02) 661994 or 526127

(In Israel, you can hear Rabbi Meir Kahane speak every Monday and Thursday evening at the above address at 8:45 PM. In the United States, if you want to arrange for him to speak in your community or get his writings or tapes contact: THE JEWISH IDEA, POB 425, Midwood Station, Brooklyn, N.Y. 11230

Distributed by
Education Department:

JDL

76 Madison Avenue
New York, N.Y. 10016
(212) 686-3041

*This Appendix is a reprint of flyers distributed by Rabbi Kahane's Kach Movement in Israel and New York.